Arabic With Husna

Arabic With Husna is a first of its kind, comprehensive Qur'anic Arabic curriculum that leverages best teaching practices based on experience with thousands of students, enhanced study materials designed to optimize student learning and most importantly video resources in order to ensure a rich, engaging, meticulously organized and result driven learning experience for children and adults alike. This curriculum was put together by a team of educators in collaboration with Ustadh Nouman Ali Khan at the Bayyinah Institute. It is hoped that this approach will revolutionize learning the language of the Qur'an for individuals and educational institutions all over the world, insha Allah.

This Arabic With Husna book is comprised of Modules, Chapters and Lessons. A module is a large, complete concept. A chapter is a subset of a module and covers an important pillar of the module. A lesson is a subset of a chapter and is the smallest piece of a concept that can be covered in one setting (e.g. in one class).

The Arabic instruction needed to complete the lessons is delivered through the Arabic With Husna series on Bayyinah TV. It is also accessible through guided explanations after each chapter. It is recommended to use both Bayyinah TV and the guided explanations for learning purposes.

To sign up for Bayyinah TV, visit www.bayyinah.tv.

Copyright © 2016 by Bayyinah Institute

All rights reserved. This book or any portion thereof may not be reproduced or used in any manner whatsoever without the express written permission of Bayyinah Institute.

Bayyinah Institute
2300 Valley View Lane, Suite 500
Irving, TX 75062

www.bayyinah.tv

ISBN: 978-0-9862750-2-9

Contributors:
Nouman Ali Khan
Aarij Anwer
Anam Bakali
Touqeer Ahmed
Faadhil AbdulHakkim
Ifrah Shareef
Naim Rahman
Hamza Baig
Merusha Nasoordeen
Javeria Khan

MODULE 2
Fragments

CHAPTER 1 — **Idhaafah**
1st of the five fragments. Word before 'of' is Mudhaaf, word after 'of' is Mudhaaf Ilayh. Rules for Idhaafah.

CHAPTER 2 — **Pronouns**
Falls under the category of Ism. Independent pronouns (always Raf' status). Attached pronouns (Nasb or Jarr status). Always proper. Other two properties are determined by meaning.

CHAPTER 3 — **Harf Jarr**
2nd of the five fragments. List of Harf Jarr to be memorized with meaning. Always make the Ism after Jarr. The fragment is called Jaar Majroor.

CHAPTER 4 — **Harf Nasb**
3rd of the five fragments. List of Harf Nasb to be memorized with meaning. Always make its Ism Nasb (doesn't have to be right after). The fragment is called Harf Nasb and its Ism.

CHAPTER 5 — **Mawsoof Sifah**
4th of the five fragments. Noun (Mawsoof)-adjective (Sifah) fragment. All four properties must match for the entire fragment. Can be more than one Sifah. Can be separated.

CHAPTER 6 — **Pointers**
5th of the five fragments. List of pointers to be memorized with meaning. Can make a fragment (must be followed by ال) or sentence (no ال after). All four properties must match for fragment.

CHAPTER 1
Idhaafah

Chapter 1

After finishing the study of the Ism, we will move on to learn how these Ism come together to form something bigger: a fragment. **A fragment is two or more words chained together by a grammar rule.**

A fragment is more than a word but less than a sentence. In other words, a fragment is bigger than a word (at least two are needed). It is not a sentence as it does not convey complete meaning. We will study five basic fragments:

1. Idhaafah الإِضَافَةُ
2. Harf Jarr الجَارُ وَالمَجْرُورُ
3. Harf Nasb حَرْفُ النَصْبِ وَاسْمُهَا
4. Mawsoof Sifah المَوْصُوفُ وَالصِّفَةُ
5. Pointers اِسْمُ الإِشَارَةِ وَ مُشَارٌ إِلَيْهِ

In this lesson we will learn about the first fragment, the Idhaafah. The Idhaafah is generally used to show possession, for example, 'the day of judgement', 'Allah's house' and 'his book.'

There are two parts to the Idhaafah fragment. The part before 'of' is called Mudhaaf (مُضَاف) and the part after 'of' is called Mudhaaf Ilayh (مُضَاف إِلَيْهِ). The Mudhaaf and Mudhaaf Ilayh together are called Idhaafah الإِضَافَةُ.

What if there is no 'of'? Sometimes, you might have to rearrange the fragment to uncover 'of'. For example, 'Allah's house' becomes 'house of Allah' and 'his book' becomes 'book of his'.

Examples

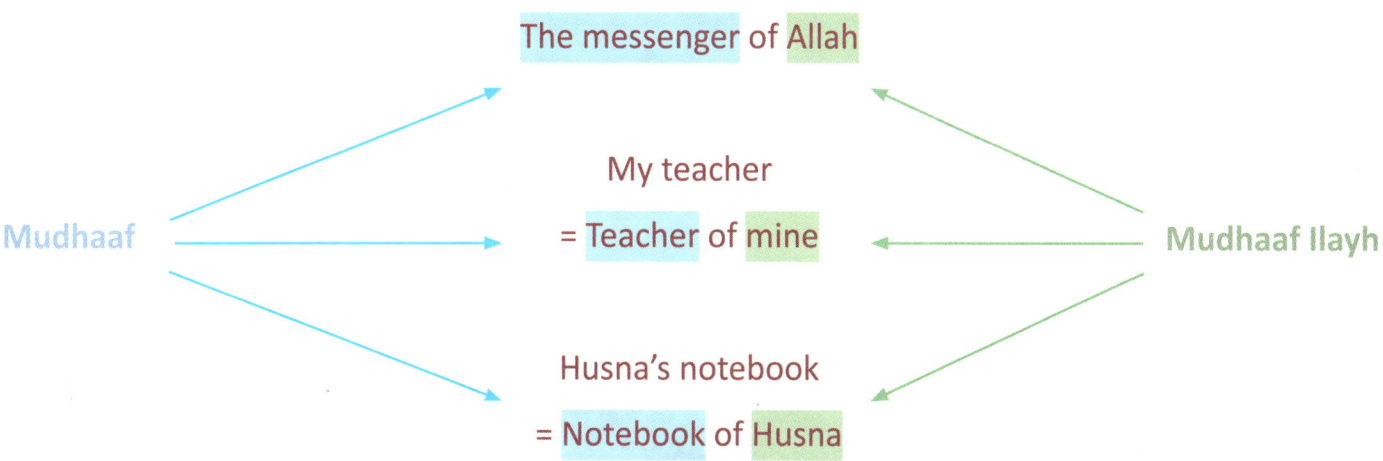

Rules fors إِضَافَة

1) The مُضَاف must be light and must not have ال.
2) The مُضَاف إِلَيْه must be in Jarr status.
3) Mudhaaf مُضَاف and Mudhaaf Ilayh مُضَاف إِلَيْه must be right next to each other.

Application

كِتَابُ اللهِ

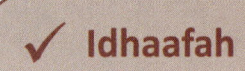 Idhaafah

- ✓ Mudhaaf is light and has no ال
- ✓ Muhdaaf Ilayh is in Jarr status
- ✓ Mudhaaf and Mudhaaf Ilayh are right next to each other

غَفُوْرٌ رَحِيْمٌ

✗ Idhaafah

- ✗ Mudhaaf is heavy

يَوْمِ نَحْسٍ

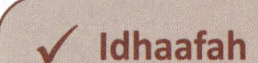 Idhaafah

- ✓ Mudhaaf is light and has no ال
- ✓ Muhdaaf Ilayh is in Jarr status
- ✓ Mudhaaf and Mudhaaf Ilayh are right next to each other

الْيَوْمِ الْمَوْعُوْدِ

✗ Idhaafah

- ✗ Mudhaaf has ال

كِتَابُ مُوْسَى

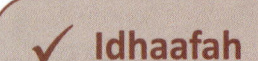 Idhaafah

- ✓ Mudhaaf is light and has no ال
- ✓ Muhdaaf Ilayh is non-flexible, so it can be in any status = counts as Jarr
- ✓ Mudhaaf and Mudhaaf Ilayh are right next to each other

جَمَعَ مَالًا

✗ Idhaafah

- ✓ Mudhaaf is light and has no ال
- ✗ Muhdaaf Ilayh is not in Jarr status

Lesson 1

Accompanying Video
Unit 1: 1.6.1

Learning Goals
• Memorize new vocabulary • Recognize Idhaafah constructions in English
• Know the rules of a Mudhaaf and Mudhaaf Ilayh

A | Watch the accompanying video. Based on what you hear and see in the video, write/circle the correct answer.

1. A fragment is something that is more than a word, but less than a _____.

2. _____ are examples of words that have a hidden 'of' (these words come after of).

   A. 'His', 'my', and 'them'   B. 'His', 'my', and 'their'   C. 'Him', 'me', and 'them'

3. Another way to find the hidden '_____' is to look for words that end with apostrophe and 's', like 'Husna's', 'Waliyah's', etc.

4. In Arabic, the part before the 'of' is called _____.

5. In Arabic, the part after the 'of' is called _____.

6. In the fragment 'Husna's notebook', Husna is the _____.

7. _____ comes between a Mudhaaf and Mudhaaf Ilayh.

8. The Mudhaaf Ilayh must be in _____ status because it comes after the 'of'.

9. The Mudhaaf must be _____ and it cannot have اَلْ.

10. _____ is an example of Mudhaaf and Mudhaaf Ilayh.

    A. غَفُوْرٌ رَحِيْمٌ   B. يَوْمٌ كَبِيْرٍ   C. يَوْمِ نَحْسٍ   D. اَلْيَوْمِ الْمَوْعُوْدِ

B | Fill in the blanks using the word bank.

> Before   More   Mine   Gender   After   Light   Jarr
> Status   Car   Mudhaaf   Fragments   Mudhaaf ilayh   Less

1. Isms have four properties: _____, number, _____, and type. Isms come together to make _____.

2. A fragment is _____ than a word but _____ then a sentence.

3. 'My car' can also be written as '_____ of _____'.

4. His, her, my, our, and your: these are all labeled '_____ of'.

5. In the fragment 'Allah's house', Allah is the part after 'of' and house is the part _____ 'of'.

6. The part before 'of' is called _____ and the part after 'of' is called _____. Together, these two parts combine to make the fragment that is called an Idhaafah.

7. The Mudhaaf has two rules: it must be _____ and cannot have اَل.

8. The Mudhaaf Ilayh must always be _____.

C | Circle the phrase that is NOT an Idhaafah.

1.	Their house	The teachers	His phone	Her hand
2.	Its goal	Our lesson	Their game	Tall buildings
3.	Messenger of Allah	Lord of the worlds	Green trees	Rising of the sun
4.	Their ears	Best friends	Our hearts	His promise
5.	That car	His problem	My computer	Our schools
6.	Shirts of mine	Promises of his	Streets of the city	Tasty food

D | Rearrange the following to read _____ of _____.

1. His slave — Slave of his

2. Their fathers

3. The orphan's treasure

4. Our Lord

5. My parents

6. The child's toy

E | Underline the Mudhaaf and circle the Mudhaaf Ilayh. Then rewrite the phrase to include 'of' if the phrase isn't already written in that format.

1. <u>Fish</u> of (the sea) _____

2. The queen's palace _____

3. Allah's house _____

4. Hijab of a girl _____

5. The building's height _____

6. Your house _____

7. Car of mine _____

8. Name of the prophet _____

9. The country's safety _____

10. Her desk _____

F | Circle the word that could be a Mudhaaf in each of the following questions. Remember the two rules that apply to every Mudhaaf.

1.	مُسْلِمٌ	اَلْمُسْلِمُ	مُسْلِمُ	11.	صَالِحَا	صَالِحَانِ	اَلصَّالِحَانِ
2.	مُسْلِماً	مُسْلِمَ	اَلْمُسْلِمَ	12.	صَالِحَيْنِ	صَالِحَيْ	اَلصَّالِحَيْنِ
3.	مُسْلِمٍ	مُسْلِمِ	اَلْمُسْلِمِ	13.	صَالِحُو	صَالِحُونَ	اَلصَّالِحُونَ
4.	مُسْلِمَا	مُسْلِمَانِ	اَلْمُسْلِمَانِ	14.	اَلصَّالِحِينَ	صَالِحِينَ	صَالِحِيْ
5.	اَلْمُسْلِمَيْنِ	مُسْلِمَيْنِ	مُسْلِمَيْ	15.	حَقِّ	عَزِيزٌ	نَفْسُ
6.	مُسْلِمُونَ	مُسْلِمُو	اَلْمُسْلِمُونَ	16.	قَلِيلاً	يَوْم	خَالِقُ
7.	اَلْمُسْلِمِينَ	مُسْلِمِينَ	مُسْلِمِيْ	17.	قَلَم	اَلْفَجْوَةِ	رِزْقٍ
8.	صَالِحٌ	صَالِحُ	اَلصَّالِحُ	18.	اَلصِّرَاطَ	اَلْغَفُورُ	مُؤْمِنِي
9.	صَالِحاً	صَالِحَ	اَلصَّالِحَ	19.	ذِكْرِ	بَاخِعٌ	رُقُودٌ
10.	اَلصَّالِحِ	صَالِحِ	صَالِحٍ	20.	اَلْبَاسِطُ	كَلِمَاتِ	اَلْقَوْمِ

Bayyinah Institute • Chapter 1

Date: _____

 **Circle the correct Arabic version of the underlined Mudhaaf. Pay attention to status and remember the two rules of a Mudhaaf.**
Hint: Remember that a doer is Raf' and a detail is Nasb.

1. We found the <u>book</u> of the teacher.
   A. كِتَاباً
   B. كِتَابٍ
   C. كِتَابَ
   D. كِتَابٌ

2. The teacher's <u>book</u> won a prize.
   A. كِتَابَ
   B. كِتَابٍ
   C. كِتَابُ
   D. كِتَابٌ

3. The teacher's <u>two books</u> sold quickly.
   A. كِتَابَانِ
   B. كِتَابٌ
   C. كِتَابَا
   D. ٱلْكِتَابَا

4. She read the teacher's <u>two books</u>.
   A. كِتَابَيْنِ
   B. كِتَابَيْ
   C. ٱلْكِتَابَا
   D. كِتَابَانِ

5. I borrowed the man's <u>pen</u>.
   A. ٱلْقَلَمِ
   B. قَلَمَ
   C. ٱلْقَلَمُ
   D. قَلَمٌ

6. The man's <u>pen</u> stopped working.
   A. قَلَمٌ
   B. ٱلْقَلَمُ
   C. قَلَمُ
   D. قَلَماً

7. The man's <u>two pens</u> fell on the ground.
   A. ٱلْقَلَمَانِ
   B. قَلَمَا
   C. قَلَمَانِ
   D. ٱلْقَلَمَيْنِ

8. I caught the man's <u>two pens</u>.
   A. قَلَمَيْنِ
   B. قَلَمَانِ
   C. قَلَمَيْ
   D. ٱلْقَلَمَا

Chapter 1 • Bayyinah Institute

Date: _____

Circle the word that could be a Mudhaaf Ilayh.

1. اَلْمُسْلِمُ   مُسْلِمَ   اَلْمُسْلِمِ   مُسْلِمٌ   مُسْلِماً

2. مُسْلِمَانِ   مُسْلِمَيْنِ   اَلْمُسْلِمَ   اَلْمُسْلِمَا   مُسْلِمٌ

3. اَلْمُسْلِمُونَ   مُسْلِمُ   مُسْلِمُونَ   مُسْلِمِي   اَلْمُسْلِمَانِ

4. مُسْلِمَةٌ   مُسْلِمَةَ   مُسْلِمَةِ   اَلْمُسْلِمَةُ   اَلْمُسْلِمَةَ

5. مُسْلِمَتَانِ   اَلْمُسْلِمَتَانِ   اَلْمُسْلِمَتَيْنِ   اَلْمُسْلِمَتَا   مُسْلِمَةَ

6. مُسْلِمَاتٌ   اَلْمُسْلِمَاتِ   مُسْلِمَاتَ   مُسْلِمَاتٍ   اَلْمُسْلِمَاتَ

7. اَلْمُسْلِمِينَ   مُسْلِمَانِ   اَلْمُسْلِمُونَ   مُسْلِمُوا   اَلْمُسْلِمَانِ

8. اَلصَّالِحِ   رِزْقاً   قَلِيلاً   خَالِقٌ   يَوْمَ

9. صَالِحَ   الْقَلَمَ   الْأَرْضَ   الصِّرَاطَ   اَلْقَلَمَ

10. اَلْمُسْلِمُ   اَلْبَاسِطُ   كَلِمَاتِ   اَلْقَوْمَ   اَلرُّعْبَ

Date: _____

Put a check next to the word if it can be a Mudhaaf or Mudhaaf Ilayh. If both words are checked off, write them together to make an Idhaafah. If not, write why not.

Hint: There are 3 reasons: اَلْ on Mudhaaf, Mudhaaf isn't light, Mudhaaf Ilayh isn't Jarr.

	Mudhaaf ilayh		Mudhaaf	
يَوْمِ الدِّينِ	اَلدِّينِ	✓	يَوْمٌ	✓	1.
	مُمَدَّدَةٍ		عَمَدٍ		2.
	اَلشِّتَاءِ		رِحْلَةَ		3.
	حَسَناً		أَجْراً		4.
	اَلرَّحِيمِ		اَلرَّحْمَانِ		5.
	مُوسَى		قَلَمٌ		6.
	اَلْمُسْلِمِينَ		أَوَّلُ		7.
	عَمَلاً		أَحْسَنُ		8.
	اَلْقَدْرِ		لَيْلَةِ		9.
	إِسْرَائِيلَ		بَنِي		10.

Lesson 2

Accompanying Video
Unit 1: 1.6.2

Learning Goals • Recognize Idhaafah constructions in English and Arabic

A | Watch the accompanying video. Based on what you hear and see in the video, write/circle the correct answer.

1. In 'The Night of Power', 'Power' is the _____.

2. In 'Their happiness', 'happiness' is the _____.

3. In 'The teacher's book', 'teacher's' is the _____.

4. In 'Your Master', 'Your' is the _____.

5. In قَوْمُ لُوطٍ, قَوْمُ is the _____.

6. عَذَابٌ أَلِيمٌ is not a Mudhaaf and Mudhaaf ilayh because _____.
   A. أَلِيمٌ is heavy   B. عَذَابٍ is heavy   C. عَذَابٍ is Jarr   D. It is a Mudhaaf and Mudhaaf Ilayh

7. أُمُّ الْقُرَى is a Mudhaaf and Mudhaaf Ilayh, true or false? _____
   A. True, all the rules apply   B. False, الْقُرَى is nasb   C. Not enough information

8. جَنَّاتُ عَدْنٍ is a Mudhaaf and Mudhaaf Ilayh, true or false? _____

9. If الْمَدِينَة means 'the city', مُسْلِمَيْ الْمَدِينَةِ means '_____'.

10. مُشْرِكُو مَكَّةَ is a Mudhaaf and Mudhaaf Ilayh: true or false? _____

Bayyinah Institute • Chapter 1

B | Fill in the blanks using the word bank.

> Before　　Fragment　　Next　　Sentence　　Light　　My　　After
> Jarr　　Car　　Mudhaaf　　Idhaafah　　Mudhaaf Ilayh　　Five

1. A _____ is more than a word but less then a _____.

2. There are _____ different fragments in Arabic. The first one you learned is called a(n) _____.

3. There are two parts in an Idhaafah: the Mudhaaf, the part _____ 'of', and the Mudhaaf Ilayh, the part _____ 'of'.

4. In the fragment 'Ali's pen', 'Ali' is the _____ and 'pen' is the _____.

5. In the fragment 'my car', '_____' is the Mudhaaf and '_____' is the Mudhaaf Ilayh.

6. The Mudhaaf has two rules: it must be _____ and cannot have اَلْ.

7. The Mudhaaf Ilayh must always be _____.

8. A Mudhaaf and its Mudhaaf Ilayh must be right _____ to each other.

16　Chapter 1　•　Bayyinah Institute

C | Determine if the fragment is an Idhaafah. If it is, circle the Mudhaaf and underline the Mudhaaf Ilayh. If not, leave it as is.

1. Fish of the sea
2. Night of Power
3. Big glass
4. Hijab of a girl
5. Messenger of Allah
6. Your house
7. Beautiful art
8. Creator of the universe
9. Your Master
10. The queen's palace
11. Their happiness
12. Fast car
13. Her desk
14. People of the Book
15. That girl
16. Car of mine
17. Our signs
18. Teacher's book
19. The country's safety
20. Their hands
21. My prayer
22. Allah's house
23. Door of the house
24. This building
25. The building's height
26. Hard lesson
27. Our pets
28. Name of the prophet
29. My desk
30. Our class

Date: _____

D
Determine if the fragment is an Idhaafah. If it is, circle the Mudhaaf and underline the Mudhaaf Ilayh. If not, leave it as is.

1. يَوْمِ الدِّينِ	11. أَصْحَابَ الكَهْفِ	21. مُشْرِكُو مَكَّةَ
2. جَمَعَ مَالاً	12. أَقَامُوا الصَّلَاةَ	22. قَلَمَا مَرْيَمَ
3. اَلسَّمَاوَاتِ وَ الْأَرْضِ	13. هَذَا البَيْتُ	23. رِحْلَةَ الشِّتَاءِ
4. قَوْمُ لُوطٍ	14. أَمَداً بَعِيداً	24. أَجْراً عَظِيماً
5. اِتَّخَذَ اللهُ	15. الرَّحْمَانِ الرَّحِيمِ	25. شَرِّ الوَسْوَاسِ
6. يَوْمَ الحَجِّ	16. رَبُّ السَّمَاوَاتِ	26. طَعَامِ المِسْكِينِ
7. أَوَّلُ المُسْلِمِينَ	17. عَذَابٌ أَلِيمٍ	27. أُمُّ القُرَى
8. أَحْسَنُ دِيناً	18. مَلِكِ النَّاسِ	28. أَهْلَ الكِتَابِ
9. أَرْبَعَةَ أَشْهُرٍ	19. لَيْلَةِ القَدْرِ	29. صُدُورَ قَوْمٍ
10. جَنَّاتُ عَدْنٍ	20. مُسْلِمَيِ المَدِينَةِ	30. بَنِي إِسْرَائِيلَ

Chapter 1 • Bayyinah Institute

Lesson 3

Date: _____

Accompanying Video
None

Learning Goals
- Know how to tell if the Mudhaaf is proper or common
- Translate Idhaafahs from English to Arabic and Arabic to English
- Identify four properties of the Mudhaaf and Mudhaaf Ilayh

A | Identify if the Mudhaaf is proper or common.
Hint: Remember that the Mudhaaf is proper if the Mudhaaf Ilayh is proper.

1. أَهْلَ الكِتَابِ   9. رَسُولُ اللهِ

2. لَيْلَةِ القَدْرِ   10. اِبْنُ مَرْيَمَ

3. رَبُّ السَّمَاوَاتِ   11. صَدِيقُ آدَمَ

4. أَكْثَرَ شَيْءٍ   12. بَيْتُ أُسْتَاذٍ

5. مَجْمَعَ البَحْرَيْنِ   13. مَلِكِ النَّاسِ

6. يَوْمِ الدِّينِ   14. رِحْلَةَ الشِّتَاءِ

7. كُلَّ سَفِينَةٍ   15. مُسْلِمَيْ مَكَّةَ

8. أَرْبَعَةَ أَشْهُرٍ   16. صُدُورَ قَوْمٍ

Bayyinah Institute • Chapter 1

B | **Translate the Idhaafahs into Arabic using the word bank. Pay attention to common and proper.**
Hint: Remember that 'the' implies that the word is proper.

House	بَيْتٌ	Door	بَابٌ	Messenger	رَسُولٌ
Pen	قَلَمٌ	Room	غُرْفَةٌ	Teacher	مُعَلِّمٌ
Allah	اَللّٰهُ	Book	كِتَابٌ	Friend	صَدِيقٌ

1. Door of the house

2. Friend of Allah

3. House of the Messenger

4. The teacher's room

5. The teacher's pen

6. The friend's pen

7. The two doors of the house

8. The teacher of the Messenger of Allah

C | **Translate the Idhaafahs into English using the word bank. Pay attention to common and proper.**
Hint: Remember that words that have ال are proper.

1. كِتَابُ اللهِ

2. بَيْتُ اللهِ

3. بَابُ الغُرْفَةِ

4. رَسُولُ اللهِ

5. بَيْتُ صَدِيقٍ

6. غُرْفَةُ بَيْتٍ

7. قَلَمَا المُعَلِّمِ

8. قَلَمُ صَدِيقٍ

9. غُرْفَتَا البَيْتِ

10. كِتَابُ صَدِيقٍ

11. بَابُ بَيْتٍ

12. بَيْتُ رَسُولِ اللهِ

BUILDING VOCABULARY — Bayyinah Institute • Chapter 1

Date: _____

D | Write the four properties of the Mudhaaf and Mudhaaf ilayh.

1. كِتَابُ اللهِ

كِتَابُ
_____ _____ _____ _____
(Status)   (Number)   (Gender)   (Type)

اللهِ
_____ _____ _____ _____
(Status)   (Number)   (Gender)   (Type)

2. كُلِّ مَثَلٍ

كُلِّ
_____ _____ _____ _____
(Status)   (Number)   (Gender)   (Type)

مَثَلٍ
_____ Singular   _____ _____
(Status)   (Number)   (Gender)   (Type)

3. يَوْمَ الحَجِّ

يَوْمَ
_____ _____ _____ _____
(Status)   (Number)   (Gender)   (Type)

الحَجِّ
_____ _____ _____ _____
(Status)   (Number)   (Gender)   (Type)

22 Chapter 1 • Bayyinah Institute

Date: _____

4. أَوَّلُ الأَوْلَادِ

أَوَّلُ
_____ _____ _____ _____
(Status)   (Number)   (Gender)   (Type)

الأَوْلَادِ
_____ _____ _____ _____
(Status)   (Number)   (Gender)   (Type)

5. قَوْمَ يُونُسَ

قَوْمَ
_____ _____ _____ _____
(Status)   (Number)   (Gender)   (Type)

يُونُسَ
_____ _____ _____ _____
(Status)   (Number)   (Gender)   (Type)

6. رِحْلَةَ الشِّتَاءِ

رِحْلَةَ
_____ Singular _____ _____
(Status)   (Number)   (Gender)   (Type)

الشِّتَاءِ
_____ _____ _____ _____
(Status)   (Number)   (Gender)   (Type)

Bayyinah Institute • Chapter 1

Important Concepts

Write the rules for a Mudhaaf and Mudhaaf Ilayh

Mudhaaf:

1. _____

2. _____

Mudhaaf Ilayh:

1. _____

Qur'anic Application

Determine whether the highlighted words are Mudhaaf or not. Write 'Yes' or 'No' under them.

تَبَارَكَ الَّذِي بِيَدِهِ الْمُلْكُ وَهُوَ عَلَىٰ كُلِّ شَيْءٍ قَدِيرٌ ۝ الَّذِي خَلَقَ الْمَوْتَ وَالْحَيَاةَ

Yes

لِيَبْلُوَكُمْ أَيُّكُمْ أَحْسَنُ عَمَلًا ۚ وَهُوَ الْعَزِيزُ الْغَفُورُ ۝ الَّذِي خَلَقَ سَبْعَ سَمَاوَاتٍ طِبَاقًا ۖ مَّا تَرَىٰ فِي خَلْقِ الرَّحْمَٰنِ مِن تَفَاوُتٍ ۖ فَارْجِعِ الْبَصَرَ هَلْ تَرَىٰ مِن فُطُورٍ ۝ ثُمَّ ارْجِعِ الْبَصَرَ كَرَّتَيْنِ يَنقَلِبْ إِلَيْكَ الْبَصَرُ خَاسِئًا وَهُوَ حَسِيرٌ ۝ وَلَقَدْ زَيَّنَّا السَّمَاءَ الدُّنْيَا بِمَصَابِيحَ وَجَعَلْنَاهَا رُجُومًا لِّلشَّيَاطِينِ ۖ وَأَعْتَدْنَا لَهُمْ عَذَابَ السَّعِيرِ ۝ وَلِلَّذِينَ كَفَرُوا بِرَبِّهِمْ عَذَابُ جَهَنَّمَ ۖ وَبِئْسَ الْمَصِيرُ ۝

CHAPTER 2
Pronouns

Chapter 2

Before continuing our study of fragments, we need to learn a new type of Ism: pronouns. In English, we have the six pronouns: he, she, they, you, I and we. In Arabic, recall that an Ism can be singular, pair or a plural. That means that there are 14 pronouns. Like all Isms, the pronouns have the four properties of the Ism. However, the pronouns have one important difference: **they do not show their status by ending sound nor by ending combination.**

There are two types of pronouns: independent pronouns and attached pronouns.

Independent Pronouns

Independent pronouns are whole words. They stand alone and do not attach themselves to another word.

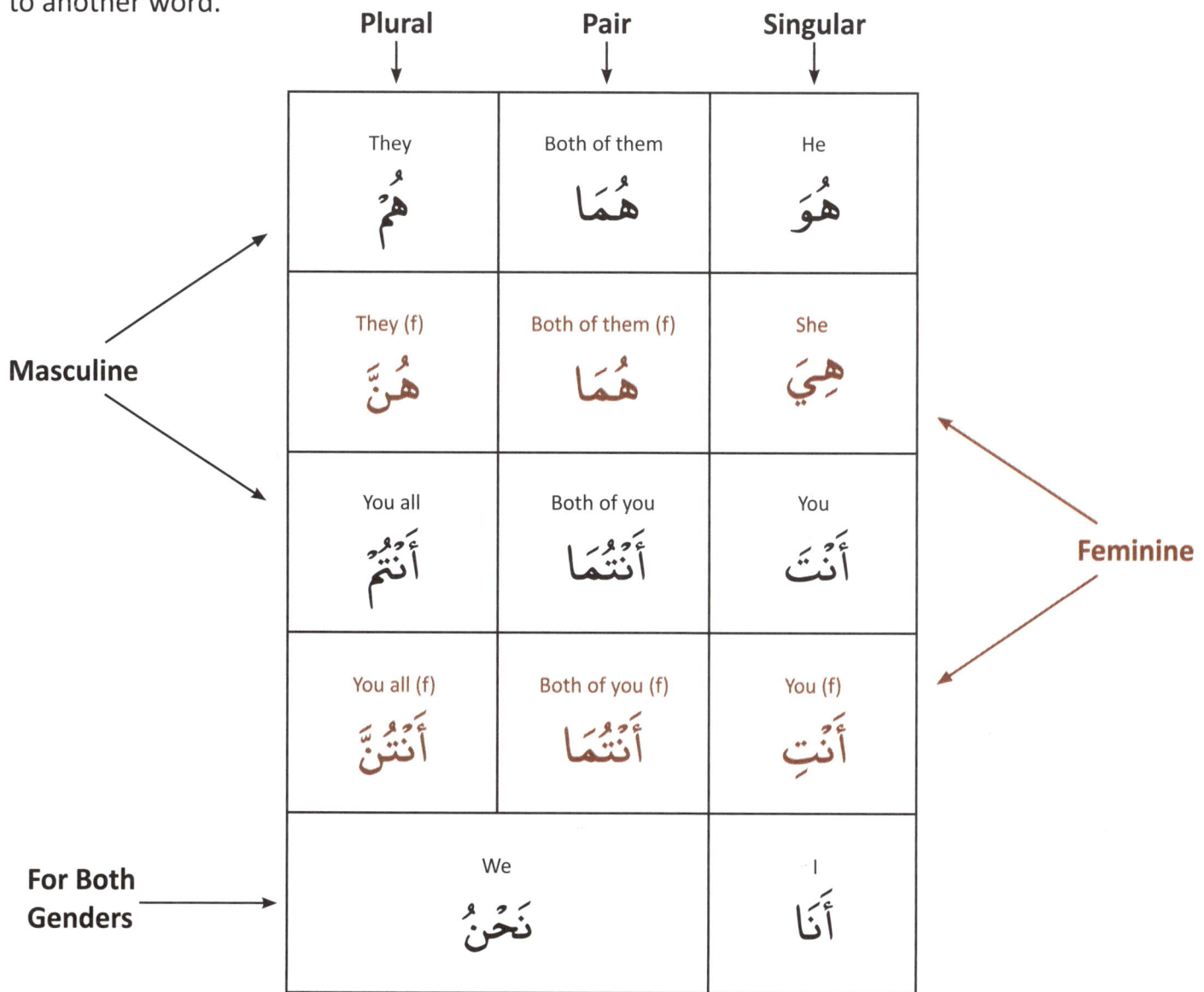

Bayyinah Institute • Chapter 2

The Four Properties of Independent Pronouns

1. Status: Always Raf'.
2. Number: Changes by the pronoun, determined by meaning.
3. Gender: Changes by the pronoun, determined by meaning.
4. Type: Always proper.

Application

Let us determine the four properties of the following pronouns:

هُوَ (He)

1. Status: Raf'
2. Number: Singular
3. Gender: Masculine
4. Type: Proper

أَنْتُنَّ (You all (f.))

1. Status: Raf'
2. Number: Plural
3. Gender: Feminine
4. Type: Proper

نَحْنُ (We)

1. Status: Raf'
2. Number: Plural
3. Gender: Masculine (Feminine if all women)
4. Type: Proper

Attached Pronouns

Attached pronouns always appear attached to another word. **Every independent pronoun has an attached version.** What can an attached pronoun be attached to? An Ism, a Fi'l, or a Harf.

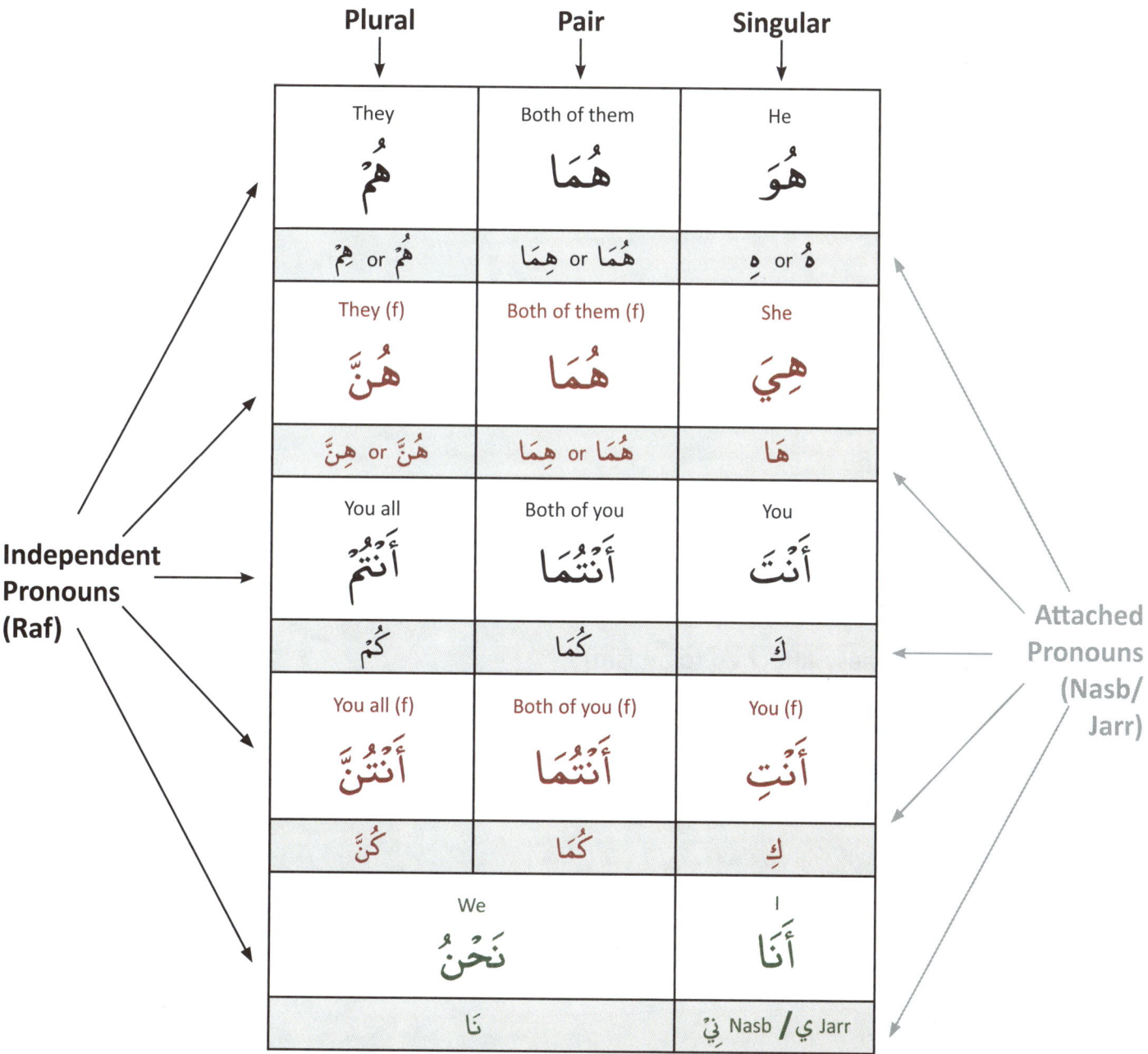

The Four Properties of Attached Pronouns

1. Status: Nasb or Jarr, determined by type of word pronoun is attached to.
2. Number: Changes by the pronoun, determined by meaning.
3. Gender: Changes by the pronoun, determined by meaning.
4. Type: Always proper.

Application

Let us determine the four properties of the following pronouns:

قَاتَلَهُمْ (He fought them)

1. Status: Nasb (because attached to a Fi'l)
2. Number: Plural
3. Gender: Masculine
4. Type: Proper

رَبُّكَ (Your master)

1. Status: Jarr (because attached to an Ism)
2. Number: Singular
3. Gender: Masculine
4. Type: Proper

عَلَيْهِمْ (On them)

1. Status: Jarr (because attached to an Harf Jarr)
2. Number: Plural
3. Gender: Masculine
4. Type: Proper

Note: هُمْ and هِمْ are the same. Their usage depends on phonetic reasons.

Status of Attached Pronouns

As you may have noticed, the status of an attached pronoun depends on the type of word the pronoun is attached to. You will learn more about this in the following chapters. Here is a handy guide to determining the status of the attached pronoun:

Attached to	Status of Pronoun	Grammar Role
Any Ism	Jarr	Mudhaaf Ilayh
Harf Jarr	Jarr	Victim of Harf Jarr
Harf Nasb	Nasb	Victim of Harf Nasb
Any Fi'l	Nasb	Maf'ool Bihi

Lesson 1

Accompanying Video
Unit 1: 1.7.1

Learning Goals • Memorize the pronouns with their meaning

A | Watch the accompanying video. Based on what you hear and see in the video, write/circle the correct answer.

1. هُوَ means '_____'.

2. هُمْ means '_____'.

3. هِيَ means '_____'.

4. أَنْتَ means '_____'.

5. أَنْتُمْ means '_____'.

6. أَنْتُمَا means '_____'.

7. أَنْتُنَّ means '_____'.

8. أَنَا means '_____'.

9. نَحْنُ means '_____'.

10. All of the above words are _____.

B | Write the pronouns in order as you learned them in the video.

هُمَا   أَنَا   أَنْتُمَا   هِيَ   هُمْ   أَنْتِ   أَنْتُنَّ
هُوَ   أَنْتَ   نَحْنُ   أَنْتُمْ   هُنَّ

C | Match each word with its meaning.

A. He

B. She

C. Both of them

D. I

E. We

F. Both of you

G. They (f)

H. All of you (f)

I. All of you

J. You

K. They

L. You (f)

1. أَنْتِ

2. أَنْتُمَا

3. هِيَ

4. نَحْنُ

5. أَنْتَ

6. هُوَ

7. هُمَا

8. أَنْتُمْ

9. هُمْ

10. أَنَا

11. هُنَّ

12. أَنْتُنَّ

BUILDING VOCABULARY

D | **Fill in the proper Arabic pronoun for each blank in the passage below.**

1. Ahmed rides the bus to school every morning. This morning, he (_____) is running late because he did not wake up on time. His mom yells up the stairs to him, "Come downstairs quickly Ahmed or you (_____) will miss the bus!" She (_____) is waiting downstairs for him with his lunch. He runs down, grabs the bag from her, and says a quick salaam over his shoulder as he (_____) runs out the door.

2. On the bus, he (_____) makes his way to the back where his two friends Yusuf and Mohammad are saving him a spot.

3. All three boys (_____) begin talking about the presentation competition that will happen in their first period class. Ahmed asks his friends, "I (_____) finished my part, did you two (_____) complete your section of the presentation?" Mohammad and Yusuf nod in unison. "We (_____) have to make sure that we (_____) win today, it is boys versus girls and we have to beat them (_____)!"

4. Once inside the classroom, they (_____) rush to unpack their bags and set up their presentation. The teacher walks past the boys saying, "I hope you all (_____) are ready to present, your group is up first."

5. The teacher makes her way to a girl sitting alone, looking worried. "What's wrong? Is everything okay with you (_____) Maryam?" Maryam tells her that both her teammates are absent today because they (_____) were not prepared for their parts. The teacher turns to Yasmeen and Rahmah saying "Both of you (_____) will work with Maryam today to prepare a presentation, and tomorrow you all (_____) will present for me."

6. The boys overhear the teacher talking to the girls. They (_____) cheer, thinking they will also not have to present today. "Settle down boys, I (_____) am only giving one group an extension. You guys (_____) are still presenting today." The boys groan and slowly make their way up to the front of the class.

E | Circle the pronoun in each question.

1.
   A. هَذَا
   B. اَلَّذِينَ
   C. فِي
   D. هُوَ

2.
   A. أَنْتَ
   B. اَلَّذِي
   C. مِلَّةَ
   D. مُكَذِّبِي

3.
   A. اَلَّتَانِ
   B. هُمْ
   C. هُمَانِ
   D. هَذِهِ

4.
   A. اَللَّاتِي
   B. أَنْتُمْ
   C. هَذَانِ
   D. أَنْتُمَانِ

5.
   A. أَنْتِنِي
   B. اَلَّذِي
   C. أَنْتُنَّ
   D. جَنَّتَانِ

6.
   A. حُبَّ
   B. هَاؤُلَاءِ
   C. اَلَّتَانِ
   D. هُنَّ

7.
   A. أَنَا
   B. صَابِرًا
   C. اَللَّذَانِ
   D. عَنْ

8.
   A. مُفْلِحُونَ
   B. هُمْ
   C. بَيْتٌ
   D. نَحْنُ

9.
   A. اَللَّتَانِ
   B. حَتَّى
   C. هِيَ
   D. اَللَّذَانِ

10.
    A. هَذَا
    B. هُمَا
    C. اَللَّاتِي
    D. عَلَى

11.
    A. أَنْتِ
    B. نَائِمُونَ
    C. رَبُّ
    D. إِلَى

12.
    A. عِنْدَ
    B. طَوْلًا
    C. جَاعِلُونَ
    D. أَنْتُمَا

Chapter 2 • Bayyinah Institute

F | Find all of the pronouns in the ayahs below.

1. إِنَّا نَحْنُ نَزَّلْنَا الذِّكْرَ وَإِنَّا لَهُ لَحَافِظُونَ ﴿٩﴾

2. قُلْ هُوَ اللَّهُ أَحَدٌ ﴿١﴾

3. فِي أَدْنَى الْأَرْضِ وَهُم مِّن بَعْدِ غَلَبِهِمْ سَيَغْلِبُونَ ﴿٣﴾

4. يُسَبِّحُ لِلَّهِ مَا فِي السَّمَاوَاتِ وَمَا فِي الْأَرْضِ ۖ لَهُ الْمُلْكُ وَلَهُ الْحَمْدُ ۖ وَهُوَ عَلَىٰ كُلِّ شَيْءٍ قَدِيرٌ ﴿١﴾

5. قَالُوا سُبْحَانَكَ لَا عِلْمَ لَنَا إِلَّا مَا عَلَّمْتَنَا ۖ إِنَّكَ أَنتَ الْعَلِيمُ الْحَكِيمُ ﴿٣٢﴾

6. وَلَا تَلْبِسُوا الْحَقَّ بِالْبَاطِلِ وَتَكْتُمُوا الْحَقَّ وَأَنتُمْ تَعْلَمُونَ ﴿٤٢﴾

7. إِلَّا الَّذِينَ تَابُوا وَأَصْلَحُوا وَبَيَّنُوا فَأُولَٰئِكَ أَتُوبُ عَلَيْهِمْ ۚ وَأَنَا التَّوَّابُ الرَّحِيمُ ﴿١٦٠﴾

8. يَوْمَ يَجْمَعُ اللَّهُ الرُّسُلَ فَيَقُولُ مَاذَا أُجِبْتُمْ ۖ قَالُوا لَا عِلْمَ لَنَا ۖ إِنَّكَ أَنتَ عَلَّامُ الْغُيُوبِ ﴿١٠٩﴾

9. قَالُوا ادْعُ لَنَا رَبَّكَ يُبَيِّن لَّنَا مَا هِيَ إِنَّ الْبَقَرَ تَشَابَهَ عَلَيْنَا وَإِنَّا إِن شَاءَ اللَّهُ لَمُهْتَدُونَ ﴿٧٠﴾

10. وَإِذْ فَرَقْنَا بِكُمُ الْبَحْرَ فَأَنجَيْنَاكُمْ وَأَغْرَقْنَا آلَ فِرْعَوْنَ وَأَنتُمْ تَنظُرُونَ ﴿٥٠﴾

Lesson 2

Date: _____

Accompanying Video
Unit 1: 1.7.2

Learning Goals • Know the grammar of pronouns • Memorize attached pronouns

A
Watch the accompanying video. Based on what you hear and see in the video, write/circle the correct answer.

1. All pronouns are always _____, so we never have to figure out their type.

2. The pronouns we have memorized so far are always _____ in status.

3. You can tell number and gender of each pronoun if you know their _____.

4. The pronouns we have memorized so far are called _____ pronouns.

5. The _____ versions of the pronouns are Nasb or Jarr.

6. The attached version of هُوَ is _____ or _____.

7. The attached version of هُمْ is _____ or _____.

8. The attached version of أَنْتَ is _____.
   A. كِ   B. كَ   C. كُمَا   D. كُمْ

9. The attached version of أَنْتُمْ is _____.
   A. كُمَا   B. كَ   C. كُنَّ   D. كُمْ

10. The Jarr attached version of أَنَا is _____.

11. The Nasb attached version of أَنَا is _____.

12. The attached version of نَحْنُ is _____.

B | Fill in the blanks using the word bank.

> Raf'   Proper   Jarr   Isms   Nasb   Singular   Attached
> Masculine   هَا   أَنْتَ   هُمْ   كَ   Meaning

1. There are two different types of pronouns: independent and _____.

2. Pronouns are _____ so they have four properties.

3. The status of independent pronouns is always _____ and the status of attached pronouns is always _____ or _____.

4. Pronouns are always _____.

5. You can tell the number and gender of pronouns by their _____. So the number and gender of هُوَ is _____ and masculine.

6. _____ is the attached version of هِيَ.

7. _____ is Raf', _____ is the Nasb/Jarr version of the same pronoun.

8. The four properties of _____ are Raf', plural, _____, and proper.

42   Chapter 2 • Bayyinah Institute

C | Match each independent pronoun to its attached version.

1. أَنْتِ
2. أَنْتُمَا
3. هِيَ
4. نَحْنُ
5. أَنْتَ
6. هُوَ
7. هُمَا
8. أَنْتُمْ
9. هُمْ
10. أَنَا
11. هُنَّ
12. أَنْتُنَّ

A. هُ/هِ
B. نَا
C. كُمْ
D. هُمَا/هِمَا
E. هُمْ/هِمْ
F. هَا
G. كِ
H. يْ/نِيْ
I. كُنَّ
J. كُمَا
K. هُنَّ/هِنَّ
L. كَ

Date: _____

D

Write the Mudhaaf, Mudhaaf Ilayh, and translation for each Idhaafah, then answer the questions below.

Translation   Mudhaaf Ilayh   Mudhaaf

1. رَبُّهُ

2. رَبَّهُ

3. رَبِّهِ

4. رَبِّي (R)

5. رَبِّي (N)

6. رَبِّي (J)

When is the attached pronoun هُ and when is it هِ?
_____

What did you learn about the attached pronoun يْ?
_____

Does the attached pronoun being هُ or هِ or the status of the Ism affect the translation?
_____

44   Chapter 2 • Bayyinah Institute

E | Write the four properties of each Ism.

Date: _____

1. رَبَّهُمْ

رَبَّ _____

(Type)   (Gender)   (Number)   (Status)

هُمْ _____

(Type)   (Gender)   (Number)   (Status)

2. رَسُولِهِ

رَسُولِ _____

(Type)   (Gender)   (Number)   (Status)

هِ _____

(Type)   (Gender)   (Number)   (Status)

3. كِتَابَكِ

كِتَابَ _____

(Type)   (Gender)   (Number)   (Status)

كِ _____

(Type)   (Gender)   (Number)   (Status)

Bayyinah Institute • Chapter 2

4. بَيْتِهِمَا

بَيْتِ
_____ _____ _____ _____
(Status)   (Number)   (Gender)   (Type)

هِمَا
_____ _____ _____ _____
(Status)   (Number)   (Gender)   (Type)

5. هِيَ
_____ _____ _____ _____
(Status)   (Number)   (Gender)   (Type)

6. أَنْتُم
_____ _____ _____ _____
(Status)   (Number)   (Gender)   (Type)

7. نَحْنُ
_____ _____ _____ _____
(Status)   (Number)   (Gender)   (Type)

8. أَنْتُنَّ
_____ _____ _____ _____
(Status)   (Number)   (Gender)   (Type)

9. أَنْتُمَا
_____ _____ _____ _____
(Status)   (Number)   (Gender)   (Type)

10. هُنَّ
_____ _____ _____ _____
(Status)   (Number)   (Gender)   (Type)

F | Write the independent version of the attached pronoun in each Idhaafah below.

1. نَفْسَكَ — أَنْتَ
2. رَبَّنَا
3. وَجْهَهُ
4. مِثْلَهُنَّ
5. أَحَدَكُمْ
6. سُرَادِقُهَا
7. كِلَاهُمَا
8. رَبُّكُمَا
9. وَالِدُكَ
10. دُونِي

11. مِثْلُكُمْ
12. رَبِّي
13. أَحَدُهُمَا
14. وَرَاءَهُمْ
15. بَرَكَاتُهُ
16. أَيْدِيَهُنَّ
17. أَمْرُكِ
18. عَيْنَاكَ
19. غَدَاءَنَا
20. كِتَابَكُمَا

Bayyinah Institute • Chapter 2 — 47

G | Find all the pronouns, independent and attached, in the ayahs below.

1. إِنَّا نَحْنُ نَزَّلْنَا الذِّكْرَ وَإِنَّا لَهُ لَحَافِظُونَ ﴿٩﴾

2. فَأَثَرْنَ بِهِ نَقْعًا ﴿٤﴾ فَوَسَطْنَ بِهِ جَمْعًا ﴿٥﴾ إِنَّ الْإِنسَانَ لِرَبِّهِ لَكَنُودٌ ﴿٦﴾ وَإِنَّهُ عَلَىٰ ذَٰلِكَ لَشَهِيدٌ ﴿٧﴾

3. فِي أَدْنَى الْأَرْضِ وَهُم مِّن بَعْدِ غَلَبِهِمْ سَيَغْلِبُونَ ﴿٣﴾

4. يُسَبِّحُ لِلَّهِ مَا فِي السَّمَاوَاتِ وَمَا فِي الْأَرْضِ ۖ لَهُ الْمُلْكُ وَلَهُ الْحَمْدُ ۖ وَهُوَ عَلَىٰ كُلِّ شَيْءٍ قَدِيرٌ ﴿١﴾

5. قَالُوا سُبْحَانَكَ لَا عِلْمَ لَنَا إِلَّا مَا عَلَّمْتَنَا ۖ إِنَّكَ أَنتَ الْعَلِيمُ الْحَكِيمُ ﴿٣٢﴾

6. وَإِذَا لَقُوا الَّذِينَ آمَنُوا قَالُوا آمَنَّا وَإِذَا خَلَوْا إِلَىٰ شَيَاطِينِهِمْ قَالُوا إِنَّا مَعَكُمْ إِنَّمَا نَحْنُ مُسْتَهْزِئُونَ ﴿١٤﴾

7. وَالَّذِينَ كَفَرُوا وَكَذَّبُوا بِآيَاتِنَا أُولَٰئِكَ أَصْحَابُ النَّارِ هُمْ فِيهَا خَالِدُونَ ﴿٣٩﴾

8. يَوْمَ يَجْمَعُ اللَّهُ الرُّسُلَ فَيَقُولُ مَاذَا أُجِبْتُمْ ۖ قَالُوا لَا عِلْمَ لَنَا ۖ إِنَّكَ أَنتَ عَلَّامُ الْغُيُوبِ ﴿١٠٩﴾

9. قَالُوا ادْعُ لَنَا رَبَّكَ يُبَيِّن لَّنَا مَا هِيَ إِنَّ الْبَقَرَ تَشَابَهَ عَلَيْنَا وَإِنَّا إِن شَاءَ اللَّهُ لَمُهْتَدُونَ ﴿٧٠﴾

10. وَإِذْ فَرَقْنَا بِكُمُ الْبَحْرَ فَأَنجَيْنَاكُمْ وَأَغْرَقْنَا آلَ فِرْعَوْنَ وَأَنتُمْ تَنظُرُونَ ﴿٥٠﴾

Lesson 3

Accompanying Video
Unit 1: 1.7.3

Learning Goals • Practice recognizing attached pronouns

A | Watch the accompanying video. Based on what you hear and see in the video, write/circle the correct answer.

1. The attached pronoun in تَحْتَكِ comes from the independent pronoun _____.

2. The attached pronoun in زِلْزَالَهَا means '_____'.

3. The attached pronoun in كَيْدَهُمْ comes from the independent pronoun _____.

4. The attached pronoun in مَوَازِينِهِ comes from the independent pronoun _____.

5. The attached pronoun in رَسُولِهِ means '_____'.

6. If you see a(n) _____ attached to a pronoun, then that _____ is a Mudhaaf and the pronoun is a Mudhaaf ilayh.

7. صَاحِبَهُمَا means '_____'.

8. نَفْسَكَ means '_____'.

9. أُمَّكِ means '_____'.

10. 'Your book' in Arabic is _____.

11. 'His pen' in Arabic is _____.

Bayyinah Institute • Chapter 2

B | Write the Mudhaaf and Mudhaaf Ilayh for each Idhaafah below.

	Mudhaaf Ilayh	Mudhaaf	
1. نَفْسَكَ	كَ	نَفْسَ	
2. كِتَابُكُمَا			
3. تَحْتَكِ			
4. صَاحِبُهُمَا			
5. زِلْزَالَهَا			
6. نَفْسَكَ			
7. كَيْدَهُمْ			
8. رَبُّكُمَا			

C | Write the independent version of the attached pronoun in each Idhaafah below, then write its meaning.

Translation	Independent pronoun	
You (masculine)	أَنْتَ	1. نَفْسَكَ
		2. مَوَازِيْنِهِ
		3. رَسُولَهُ
		4. أَشَدَّهُمَا
		5. أُمَّهُمْ
		6. آيَاتِنَا
		7. عَهْدِكُمْ
		8. أَحَدُكُمَا
		9. أَفْوَاهِهِمْ
		10. عَبْدِهِ

Date: _____

	Translation	Independent pronoun	
11. آثارِهِمْ	They	هُمْ	
12. رَبَّنَا			
13. دَعْوَتُكُمَا			
14. أَمْرِنَا			
15. كَيْدِكُنَّ			
16. وَلَدِهَا			
17. ذَنْبِكِ			
18. أَوْلَادَهُنَّ			
19. آذَانِهِمْ			
20. أَيْدِيَهُمَا			

Chapter 2 • Bayyinah Institute

D | Translate the Idhaafahs into Arabic using the word bank. Keep the Mudhaaf in Raf' status for this exercise.

House	بَيْتٌ	Door	بَابٌ	Messenger	رَسُولٌ
Pen	قَلَمٌ	Room	غُرْفَةٌ	Teacher	مُعَلِّمٌ
Allah	اَللَّهُ	Book	كِتَابٌ	Friend	صَدِيقٌ

1. Her house

2. My friend

3. Their (2) book

4. Your (pl) teacher

5. Our Messenger

6. Your (f) room

7. My friend's teacher

8. The pen of my teacher

E

Translate the Idhaafahs into English using the word bank. Pay attention to common and proper.

Hint: Remember that words that have اَلْ are proper.

1. كِتَابُكُمَا

2. بَابُهُمْ

3. غُرْفَتُكُنَّ

4. رَسُولِي

5. بَيْتُنَا

6. غُرْفَتُهَا

7. مُعَلِّمِي

8. مُعَلِّمَاهُنَّ

9. بَيْتُ صَدِيقِهِمَا

10. مُعَلِّمُ رَسُولِنَا

11. كِتَابُ صَدِيقَتِهِمْ

12. بَابُ غُرْفَتِنَا

F | Write the four properties of each ism.

Date: _____

1. كَهْفِهِمْ

كَهْفِ

_____ _____ _____ _____
(Status)   (Number)   (Gender)   (Type)

هِمْ

_____ _____ _____ _____
(Status)   (Number)   (Gender)   (Type)

2. جَنَّتَهُ

جَنَّتَ

_____ _____ _____ _____
(Status)   (Number)   (Gender)   (Type)

هُ

_____ _____ _____ _____
(Status)   (Number)   (Gender)   (Type)

3. عَيْنَاكَ

عَيْنَا

_____ _____ _____ _____
(Status)   (Number)   (Gender)   (Type)

كَ

_____ _____ _____ _____
(Status)   (Number)   (Gender)   (Type)

Bayyinah Institute • Chapter 2

G | Make an Idaafah with the word and the given pronoun.

1. عَمَلٌ   عَمَلُهُ (هُوَ)   _____ (هُمَا)   _____ (هُمْ)

2. كِتَابٍ   _____ (هِيَ)   _____ (هُمَا)   _____ (هُنَّ)

3. البَيْتَ   _____ (أَنْتَ)   _____ (أَنْتُمَا)   _____ (أَنْتُمْ)

4. رَبُّ   _____ (أَنْتِ)   _____ (أَنْتُمَا)   _____ (أَنْتُنَّ)

5. وَلَدٍ   _____ (أَنَا)   _____ (نَحْنُ)

H. Identify if the fragment is an Idaafah. If it isn't, write why not.

1. حَذَرَ الْمَوْتِ — Yes / No
2. عَذَابٌ عَظِيمٌ — Yes / No
3. ذَٰلِكَ الْكِتَابُ — Yes / No
4. خَتَمَ اللَّهُ — Yes / No
5. يَدْخُلَ الْجَنَّةَ — Yes / No
6. اَلدَّارُ الْآخِرَةُ — Yes / No
7. دَارُ الْآخِرَةِ — Yes / No
8. وَقُودُهَا — Yes / No
9. آمَنَ السُّفَهَاءُ — Yes / No
10. أَنْتَ الْعَلِيمُ — Yes / No

Bayyinah Institute • Chapter 2

Date: _____

Important Concepts

Write the status of the pronoun:

1. Independent pronouns: _____

2. Pronoun attached to an Ism: _____

3. Pronoun attached to a Fi'l: _____

Qur'anic Application

Circle all of the independent pronouns and underline all of the attached pronouns.

تَبَارَكَ الَّذِي بِيَدِهِ الْمُلْكُ وَهُوَ عَلَىٰ كُلِّ شَيْءٍ قَدِيرٌ ﴿١﴾ الَّذِي خَلَقَ الْمَوْتَ وَالْحَيَاةَ لِيَبْلُوَكُمْ أَيُّكُمْ أَحْسَنُ عَمَلًا ۚ وَهُوَ الْعَزِيزُ الْغَفُورُ ﴿٢﴾ الَّذِي خَلَقَ سَبْعَ سَمَاوَاتٍ طِبَاقًا ۖ مَّا تَرَىٰ فِي خَلْقِ الرَّحْمَٰنِ مِن تَفَاوُتٍ ۖ فَارْجِعِ الْبَصَرَ هَلْ تَرَىٰ مِن فُطُورٍ ﴿٣﴾ ثُمَّ ارْجِعِ الْبَصَرَ كَرَّتَيْنِ يَنقَلِبْ إِلَيْكَ الْبَصَرُ خَاسِئًا وَهُوَ حَسِيرٌ ﴿٤﴾ وَلَقَدْ زَيَّنَّا السَّمَاءَ الدُّنْيَا بِمَصَابِيحَ وَجَعَلْنَاهَا رُجُومًا لِّلشَّيَاطِينِ ۖ وَأَعْتَدْنَا لَهُمْ عَذَابَ السَّعِيرِ ﴿٥﴾ وَلِلَّذِينَ كَفَرُوا بِرَبِّهِمْ عَذَابُ جَهَنَّمَ ۖ وَبِئْسَ الْمَصِيرُ ﴿٦﴾

CHAPTER 3
Harf Jarr

Chapter 3

The Jaar Majroor الجَارُ وَ المَجْرُوْر is comprised of two parts:

1. **Harf Jarr:** Recall that a Harf is a word that makes no sense unless a word comes after it. A Harf Jarr is a Harf. What comes after it? An Ism. What role does a Harf Jarr play? It puts the Ism after it in Jarr status.

2. **Ism Majroor:** This is the Ism in Jarr status that comes right after the Harf Jarr. Nothing can come between the Harf of Jarr and its Ism.

The Harf Jarr (also called Jaar) and Ism Majroor (also called Majroor) together are called the Jaar Majroor الجَارُ وَ المَجْرُوْر fragment.

The Harf Jarr

There are 17 Harf Jarr in Arabic, but our focus is on the 11 that appear in the Qur'an:

بِ	تَ	كَ	لَ / لِ	وَ	
With	I swear by Allah	Like	For	I swear by	
مِنْ	فِيْ	عَنْ	عَلَى	حَتَّى	إِلَى
From	In	About	On	Until	To

Examples

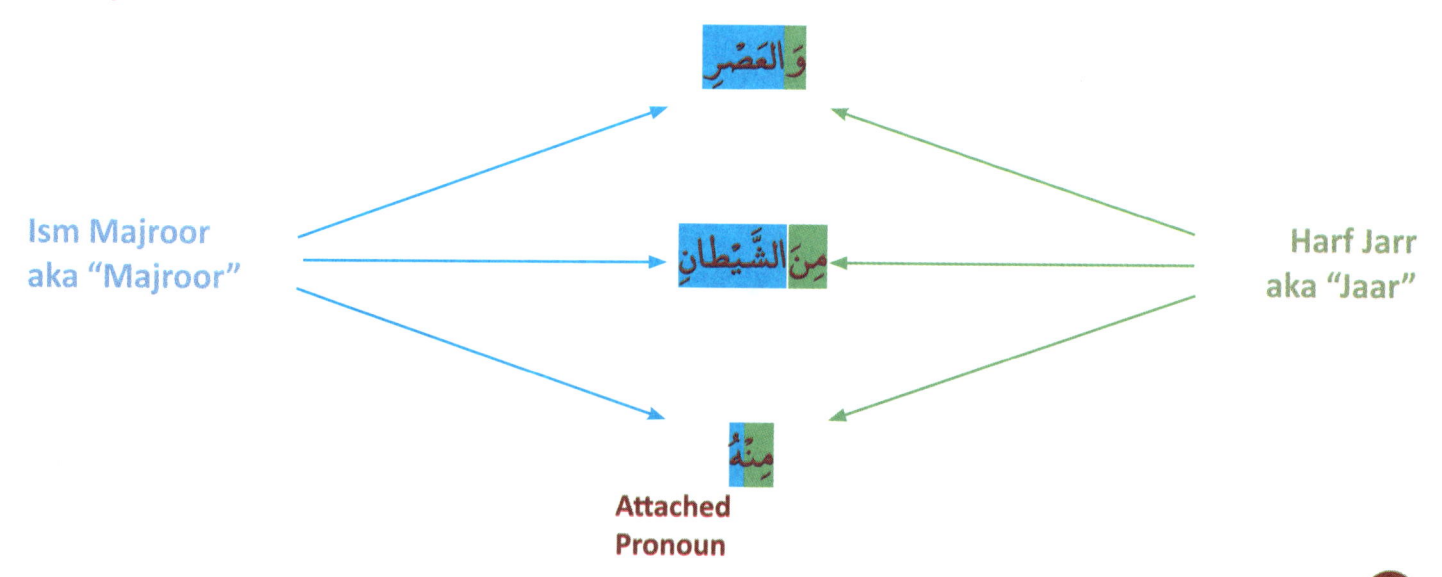

Ism Majroor aka "Majroor" — وَالْعَصْرِ — **Harf Jarr aka "Jaar"**

مِنَ الشَّيْطَانِ

مِنْهُ

Attached Pronoun

Lesson 1

Accompanying Video
Unit 1: 1.8.1

Learning Goals • Memorize the Harf Jarr with their meaning

A
Watch the accompanying video. Based on what you hear and see in the video, write/circle the correct answer.

1. بِ, تَ, _____, لَ, _____, مِنْ, فِي, _____, عَلَى, حَتَّى, إِلَى

2. The words above are called _____.

3. A Harf is a word that makes no sense unless _____.

4. A Harf has _____ properties.

5. The job of a Harf Jarr is to make sure that the word that comes after it is _____.

6. The Harf Jarr is called the _____ and its victim is called the _____.
   A. Majroor/Jaar   B. Harf of Jarr/Jaar   C. Jaar/Majroor   D. Jaar/Harf of Jarr

7. In لِرَبِّكَ, the word لِ is the Jaar, رَبِّ is the _____, رَبِّ is also a Mudhaaf, and كَ is the Mudhaaf Ilayh.

8. بِ always gets pronounced بِ (with a kasrah) and it means '_____'.

9. لَ is written as لَ when it comes with a pronoun and as لِ when it comes with anything else, it means '_____'.

10. وَ means '_____', it's tricky like لَ because there are different kinds of وَ.

Bayyinah Institute • Chapter 3

B | Fill in the blanks using the word bank.

> Majroor Jaar Fragment Jobs Four Three
> Jarr Harf اَللَّهِ بِ لَ لِ Fi'l

1. There are _____ types of words in Arabic: Ism, _____, and Harf.

2. A _____ is a word that makes no sense unless a word comes after it.

3. A(n) Ism has _____ properties. A Harf doesn't have properties, they have _____.

4. A Harf Jarr plus its victim is a type of _____.

5. The job of a Harf Jarr is to make the word after it _____.

6. When a Harf Jarr is beating up another word, it is called a _____. The word that it's beating up is called the _____.

7. In the fragment بِاللَّهِ, _____ is the Jaar and _____ is the Majroor.

8. The Harf Jarr لِ is _____ when it comes with a pronoun and _____ when it comes with anything else.

Chapter 3 • Bayyinah Institute

C | Write the Harfs Jarr in order as you learned them in the video.

عَنْ   تَ   فِي   كَ   إِلَى   مِنْ   حَتَّى
بِ   عَلَى   ل   وَ

_____   _____   _____   _____   _____

_____   _____   _____   _____   _____

D | Match the Harf with its meaning.

A. Like   1. بِ

B. I swear by Allah   2. لَ/لِ

C. With   3. تَ

D. I swear by   4. وَ

E. For   5. كَ

E

When the Harf Jarr ل is attached to a pronoun, it's read لَ. Attach the correct version of the harf to the pronoun or the Ism after it. For questions 13-24, add the correct harakaat to the end of the word.

1. ل + هُ = _____
2. ل + هُمَا = _____
3. ل + هُمْ = _____
4. ل + هَا = _____
5. ل + هُنَّ = _____
6. ل + كَ = _____
7. ل + كُمَا = _____
8. ل + كُمْ = _____
9. ل + كِ = _____
10. ل + كُنَّ = _____
11. ل + نَا = _____
12. ل + ي = _____

13. ل + مُسْلِم = _____
14. ل + المُسْلِم = _____
15. ل + صَدِيقَة = _____
16. ل + الصَّدِيقَة = _____
17. ل + مُعَلِّم = _____
18. ل + المُعَلِّم = _____
19. ل + مَدْرَسَة = _____
20. ل + المَدْرَسَة = _____
21. ل + مُوسَى = _____
22. ل + الله = _____
23. ل + مُحَمَّد = _____
24. ل + مَكَّة = _____

F | Find all of the Harf Jarr in the ayahs below.

1. إِنَّا أَرْسَلْنَا نُوحًا إِلَىٰ قَوْمِهِ أَنْ أَنذِرْ قَوْمَكَ مِن قَبْلِ أَن يَأْتِيَهُمْ عَذَابٌ أَلِيمٌ ﴿١﴾

2. يَوْمَ يُكْشَفُ عَن سَاقٍ وَيُدْعَوْنَ إِلَى السُّجُودِ فَلَا يَسْتَطِيعُونَ ﴿٤٢﴾

3. إِلَّا طَرِيقَ جَهَنَّمَ خَالِدِينَ فِيهَا أَبَدًا ۚ وَكَانَ ذَٰلِكَ عَلَى اللَّهِ يَسِيرًا ﴿١٦٩﴾

4. ثُمَّ بَدَا لَهُم مِّن بَعْدِ مَا رَأَوُا الْآيَاتِ لَيَسْجُنُنَّهُ حَتَّىٰ حِينٍ ﴿٣٥﴾

5. إِنَّا أَرْسَلْنَاكَ بِالْحَقِّ بَشِيرًا وَنَذِيرًا ۚ وَإِن مِّنْ أُمَّةٍ إِلَّا خَلَا فِيهَا نَذِيرٌ ﴿٢٤﴾

6. الَّذِي يُوَسْوِسُ فِي صُدُورِ النَّاسِ ﴿٥﴾ مِنَ الْجِنَّةِ وَالنَّاسِ ﴿٦﴾

7. وَالْعَصْرِ ﴿١﴾ إِنَّ الْإِنسَانَ لَفِي خُسْرٍ ﴿٢﴾

8. أَلَمْ تَرَ كَيْفَ فَعَلَ رَبُّكَ بِأَصْحَابِ الْفِيلِ ﴿١﴾ أَلَمْ يَجْعَلْ كَيْدَهُمْ فِي تَضْلِيلٍ ﴿٢﴾

9. فَسَبِّحْ بِحَمْدِ رَبِّكَ وَاسْتَغْفِرْهُ ۚ إِنَّهُ كَانَ تَوَّابًا ﴿٣﴾

10. أَلَمْ نَشْرَحْ لَكَ صَدْرَكَ ﴿١﴾ وَوَضَعْنَا عَنكَ وِزْرَكَ ﴿٢﴾

Bayyinah Institute • Chapter 3

Lesson 2

Accompanying Video
Unit 1: 1.8.2

Learning Goals • Learn how to attach certain Harf Jarr to pronouns and other Isms

A
Watch the accompanying video. Based on what you hear and see in the video, write/circle the correct answer.

1. كَ means '_____' and لِ means 'for' (not the number four).

2. مِنْ means '_____' and when it is followed by the word اللّٰه or any other word with ال, you put a fathah on the ن to connect the two words (e.g. مِنَ اللّٰهِ).

3. فِي means '_____' and doesn't change at all.

4. عَنْ means '_____' and does the same thing as مِنْ, except that it takes a kasrah (e.g. عَنِ اللّٰهِ).

5. عَلَى means '_____' and is pronounced عَلَيْ when a pronoun is attached to it (e.g. عَلَيْكُمْ).

6. حَتَّى means '_____' and doesn't change at all.

7. إِلَى means '_____' and is pronounced إِلَيْ when a pronoun is attached to it (e.g. إِلَيْنَا).

8. تَ means '_____' and is only used with the word اللّٰه.

9. لِ means '_____'.

B | Fill in the blanks using the word bank.

> Fragment   After   Sentence   Four   Fi'l   Zero
> Jaar   Ism   Jarr   Majroor   Harf

1. A(n) _____ is more than a word but less then a(n) _____.

2. There are three kinds of words in Arabic: Ism, Fi'l, and_____.

3. A(n) _____ is a person, place, thing, idea, adjective, adverb, and more.

4. A(n) _____ is a word that is stuck in the past, present, or future tense.

5. A Harf is a word that makes no sense unless another word comes _____ it.

6. An Ism has _____ properties, but a Harf has _____ properties.

7. An Ism after a Harf Jarr is in _____ status.

8. A Harf Jarr is called the _____ and the word it affects is called the _____.

C | Match the word with its meaning, then write the Harfs in order on the lines below.

Date: _____

A. With   1. فِي

B. From   2. لَ/لِ

C. On/Upon   3. بِ

D. In   4. مِنْ/مِنَ

E. For   5. وَ

F. Like   6. كَ

G. I swear by   7. عَنْ/عَنِ

H. Until   8. عَلَى/عَلَيَّ

I. To   9. تَ

J. I swear by Allah   10. إِلَى/إِلَيَّ

K. About   11. حَتَّى

_____ _____ _____ _____ _____

_____ _____ _____ _____ _____

BUILDING VOCABULARY

D

When the Harfs عَلى and إلى attach to a pronoun, they turn into عَلَيَّ and إلَيَّ. Attach the correct version of each Harf to the pronoun or the Ism after it. For questions 11-20, also add the correct harakaat to the end of the word.

1. إلى + هُ = إلَيْهِ
2. عَلى + هُمْ = عَلَيْهِمْ
3. إلى + ها = إلَيْها
4. عَلى + هُنَّ = عَلَيْهِنَّ
5. إلى + كَ = إلَيْكَ
6. عَلى + كُمْ = عَلَيْكُمْ
7. إلى + كِ = إلَيْكِ
8. عَلى + نا = عَلَيْنا
9. إلى + ي = إلَيَّ
10. عَلى + ي = عَلَيَّ

11. إلى + مَسْجِد = إلى مَسْجِدٍ
12. عَلى + المَسْجِد = عَلى المَسْجِدِ
13. إلى + طاوِلَة = إلى طاوِلَةٍ
14. عَلى + الطَّاوِلَة = عَلى الطَّاوِلَةِ
15. إلى + بَيْت = إلى بَيْتٍ
16. عَلى + البَيْت = عَلى البَيْتِ
17. إلى + سَفَر = إلى سَفَرٍ
18. عَلى + السَّفَر = عَلى السَّفَرِ
19. إلى + الله = إلى اللهِ
20. عَلى + الله = عَلى اللهِ

E

When the Harfs عَنْ and مِنْ come before an Ism that has ال, they turn into عَنِ and مِنَ. Attach the correct version of each Harf to the pronoun or the Ism after it.

1. مِنْ + هُ = _____
2. مِنْ + هُمْ = _____
3. مِنْ + كَ = _____
4. مِنْ + كُمْ = _____
5. مِنْ + نَا = _____
6. مِنْ + ني = _____
7. مِنْ + بَيْت = _____
8. مِنْ + البَيْت = _____
9. مِنْ + وَلَد = _____
10. مِنْ + الوَلَد = _____

11. عَنْ + هَا = _____
12. عَنْ + هُمَا = _____
13. عَنْ + كِ = _____
14. عَنْ + كُنَّ = _____
15. عَنْ + نَا = _____
16. عَنْ + ني = _____
17. عَنْ + بَيْت = _____
18. عَنْ + البَيْت = _____
19. عَنْ + وَلَد = _____
20. عَنْ + الوَلَد = _____

Bayyinah Institute • Chapter 3

F | Circle the correct version of each fragment.
Hint: Remember that a word after a Harf Jarr must be in Jarr status.

1. A. فِي بَيْتٌ
   B. فِي بَيْتاً
   C. فِي بَيْتٍ

2. A. عَلَى الكِتَابِ
   B. عَلَى الكِتَابُ
   C. عَلَى الكِتَابَ

3. A. عَنْ صَدِيقٌ
   B. عَنْ صَدِيقٍ
   C. عَنْ صَدِيقاً

4. A. بِرَسُولٍ
   B. بِرَسُولاً
   C. بِرَسُولٌ

5. A. مِنَ الغُرْفَةَ
   B. مِنَ الغُرْفَةُ
   C. مِنَ الغُرْفَةِ

6. A. تَاللهِ
   B. تَاللهُ
   C. تَاللهَ

7. A. حَتَّى مَطْلَعُ
   B. حَتَّى مَطْلَعِ
   C. حَتَّى مَطْلَعَ

8. A. كَعَصْفاً
   B. كَعَصْفٌ
   C. كَعَصْفٍ

9. A. مِنَ المُسْلِمِينِ
   B. مِنَ المُسْلِمُونَ
   C. مِنَ المُسْلِمِينَ

10. A. إِلَى مُوسَى
    B. إِلَى مُوسَيْ
    C. إِلَى مُوسِي

11. A. إِلَى يُوسُفِ
    B. إِلَى يُوسُفُ
    C. إِلَى يُوسُفَ

12. A. لِلْمُعَلِّمُ
    B. لِلْمُعَلِّمِ
    C. لِلْمُعَلِّمَ

Lesson 3

Accompanying Video
Unit 1: 1.8.3

Learning Goals • Identify, translate, and label Harf Jarr and Idhaafah fragments

A | Watch the accompanying video. Based on what you hear and see in the video, write/circle the correct answer.

1. In all of Arabic, there are only two reasons for a word to be Jarr, either it's a Harf Jarr that beats it up or it's a _____ that beats it up.

2. In بِرَبِّ الفَلَقِ, the word بِ is the Harf Jarr, رَبِّ is the Majroor, رَبِّ is also a Mudhaaf, and الفَلَقِ is the _____.

3. In رَبُّكَ, the word كَ cannot be a Harf Jarr because a Harf Jarr only comes at the beginning of a word, never at the end. The كَ in رَبُّكَ is an attached _____.

4. In كَيْدَهُمْ, the word هُمْ is the _____.

5. In عَلَيْهِمْ, the word هِمْ is the _____.

6. In بِالدِّينِ, the word بِ is the _____.

7. In عَلَى طَعَامِ المِسْكِينِ, the word طَعَامِ is the Majroor and it also the _____.

8. In صَلَاتِهِمْ, the word هِمْ is the _____.

9. In بِيَدِهِ, the word هِ is the _____.

10. In إِلَيْكَ, the word إِلَى is the _____.

Bayyinah Institute • Chapter 3

B | **Determine if each fragment is an Idhaafah or a Harf Jarr fragment. Circle the correct answer, then break down the fragment into its two parts.**

Majroor/Mudhaaf Ilayh	Jaar/Mudhaaf			
البَيْتِ	إِلَى	Harf Jarr	Idhaafah	1. إِلَى البَيْتِ
		Harf Jarr	Idhaafah	2. كَيْدَهُمْ
		Harf Jarr	Idhaafah	3. وَالتِّينِ
		Harf Jarr	Idhaafah	4. بِالحَقِّ
		Harf Jarr	Idhaafah	5. فِي الدُّنْيَا
		Harf Jarr	Idhaafah	6. عَلَى اللَّهِ
		Harf Jarr	Idhaafah	7. إِلَيْهِمْ
		Harf Jarr	Idhaafah	8. رَبُّكَ

C | Translate each of the following fragments into Arabic using the word bank.

House	بَيْتٌ	Door	بَابٌ	Messenger	رَسُولٌ
Pen	قَلَمٌ	Room	غُرْفَةٌ	Teacher	مُعَلِّمٌ
Allah	اَللَّهُ	Book	كِتَابٌ	Friend	صَدِيقٌ

1. On it

2. To the house

3. In the room

4. For my friend

5. About a book

6. From her room

7. Like your friend

8. With my teacher's book

D | Translate each of the following fragments into English using the word bank. Pay attention to common and proper.

1. عَنْهُمْ

2. مِنْهُمَا

3. عَلَيْكُمْ

4. فِيهِ

5. بِي

6. كَقَلَمٍ

7. لِلرَّسُولِ

8. مِنَ الْمُعَلِّمَيْنِ

9. لِقَلَمَيْنِ

10. مَعَ صَدِيقَتِكِ

11. فِي كِتَابِ اللهِ

12. إِلَى بَيْتِ صَدِيقِهِمَا

E

In each of the following combined fragments, write out the Jaar and Majroor in the first column, then write the Mudhaaf and Mudhaaf Ilayh in the second column.

عَبْدِهِ	عَلَىٰ عَبْدِ	1. عَلَىٰ عَبْدِهِ
		2. مِنْ لَدُنْهُ
		3. عَنْ كَهْفِهِمْ
		4. عَلَىٰ قُلُوبِهِمْ
		5. بِوَرِقِكُمْ
		6. فِي مِلَّتِهِمْ
		7. مِنْ أَفْوَاهِهِمْ
		8. لِأَنْفُسِهِمْ
		9. فِي جَوِّ السَّمَاءِ
		10. بِاسْمِ اللَّهِ

F — Label the underlined fragments as 'Harf Jarr' or 'Idhaafah'.

بِسْمِ اللَّهِ الرَّحْمَٰنِ الرَّحِيمِ

قُلْ أَعُوذُ بِرَبِّ الْفَلَقِ ۝١ مِن شَرِّ مَا خَلَقَ ۝٢ وَمِن شَرِّ غَاسِقٍ إِذَا وَقَبَ ۝٣

وَمِن شَرِّ النَّفَّاثَاتِ فِي الْعُقَدِ ۝٤ وَمِن شَرِّ حَاسِدٍ إِذَا حَسَدَ ۝٥

بِسْمِ اللَّهِ الرَّحْمَٰنِ الرَّحِيمِ

أَلَمْ تَرَ كَيْفَ فَعَلَ رَبُّكَ بِأَصْحَابِ الْفِيلِ ۝١ أَلَمْ يَجْعَلْ كَيْدَهُمْ فِي تَضْلِيلٍ ۝٢

وَأَرْسَلَ عَلَيْهِمْ طَيْرًا أَبَابِيلَ ۝٣ تَرْمِيهِم بِحِجَارَةٍ مِّن سِجِّيلٍ ۝٤

فَجَعَلَهُمْ كَعَصْفٍ مَّأْكُولٍ ۝٥

Qur'anic Application

Circle all of the Harfs Jarr below.

تَبَارَكَ الَّذِي بِيَدِهِ الْمُلْكُ وَهُوَ عَلَىٰ كُلِّ شَيْءٍ قَدِيرٌ ﴿١﴾ الَّذِي خَلَقَ الْمَوْتَ وَالْحَيَاةَ لِيَبْلُوَكُمْ أَيُّكُمْ أَحْسَنُ عَمَلًا ۚ وَهُوَ الْعَزِيزُ الْغَفُورُ ﴿٢﴾ الَّذِي خَلَقَ سَبْعَ سَمَاوَاتٍ طِبَاقًا ۖ مَّا تَرَىٰ فِي خَلْقِ الرَّحْمَٰنِ مِن تَفَاوُتٍ ۖ فَارْجِعِ الْبَصَرَ هَلْ تَرَىٰ مِن فُطُورٍ ﴿٣﴾ ثُمَّ ارْجِعِ الْبَصَرَ كَرَّتَيْنِ يَنقَلِبْ إِلَيْكَ الْبَصَرُ خَاسِئًا وَهُوَ حَسِيرٌ ﴿٤﴾ وَلَقَدْ زَيَّنَّا السَّمَاءَ الدُّنْيَا بِمَصَابِيحَ وَجَعَلْنَاهَا رُجُومًا لِّلشَّيَاطِينِ ۖ وَأَعْتَدْنَا لَهُمْ عَذَابَ السَّعِيرِ ﴿٥﴾ وَلِلَّذِينَ كَفَرُوا بِرَبِّهِمْ عَذَابُ جَهَنَّمَ ۖ وَبِئْسَ الْمَصِيرُ ﴿٦﴾

CHAPTER 4
Harf Nasb

Chapter 4

The Harf Nasb حَرْفُ النَّصْبِ fragment is comprised of two parts:

1) Harf Nasb: Recall that a Harf is a word that makes no sense unless a word comes after it. A Harf Nasb is a Harf that puts its victim Ism in Nasb status.

2) Victim: This is the Ism in Nasb status that comes after the Harf Nasb. **It does not have to be immediately after the Harf Nasb.**

The Harf Nasb

إِنَّ	أَنَّ	كَأَنَّ	لَيْتَ
For sure, certainly	That	As though	If only
لَكِنَّ	لَعَلَّ	بِأَنَّ	لِأَنَّ
However	Perhaps, hopefully, so that	Because	Because

Examples

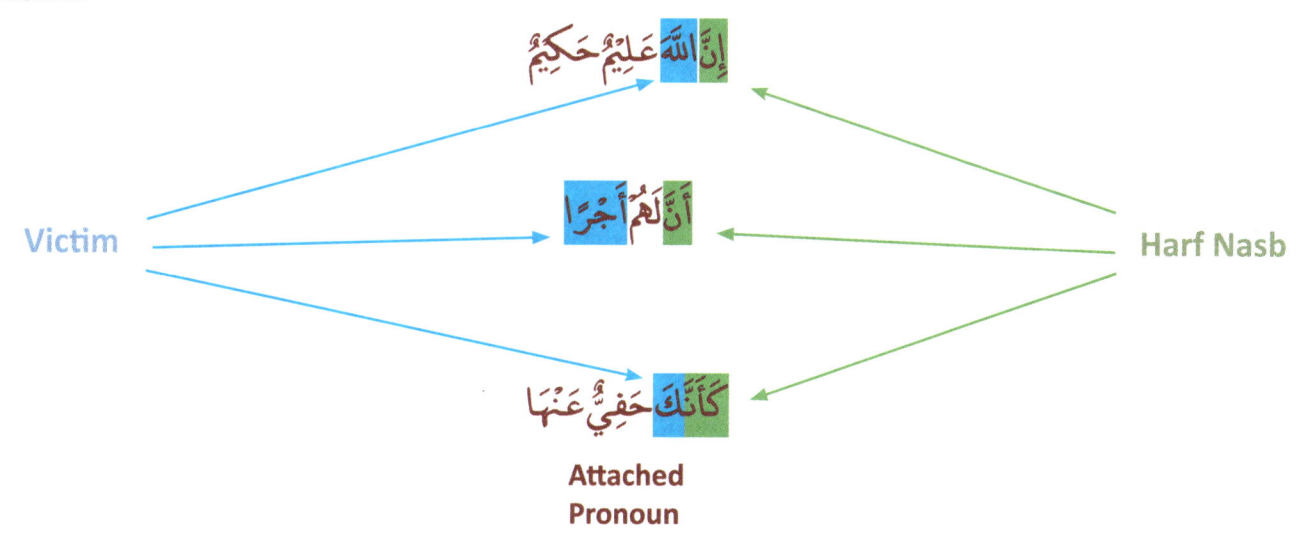

إِنَّ اللهَ عَلِيمٌ حَكِيمٌ

أَنَّ لَهُمْ أَجْرًا

كَأَنَّكَ حَفِيٌّ عَنْهَا (Attached Pronoun)

Victim ← → Harf Nasb

Tip: Simply look for the first Ism in the Nasb status after the Harf Nasb. That will be the victim.

Lesson 1

Accompanying Video
Unit 1: 1.9.1

Learning Goals • Memorize the Harf Nasb with their meaning

A | **Watch the accompanying video. Based on what you hear and see in the video, write/circle the correct answer.**

1. The first fragment we learned was _____ and Mudhaaf Ilayh.

2. The second fragment we learned was _____ and its victim.

3. The third fragment we will learn is _____ and its victim.

4. إِنَّ means '_____'.

5. أَنَّ means '_____'.

6. كَأَنَّ means '_____'.

7. لَيْتَ means '_____'.

8. لَكِنَّ means '_____'.

9. لَعَلَّ means three things: '_____', '_____', '_____'.

Bayyinah Institute • Chapter 4

B | Write the Harf Nasb in order as you learned them in the video.

لَيْتَ   لَعَلَّ   كَأَنَّ   إِنَّ   لَكِنَّ   أَنَّ

_____ _____ _____ _____ _____ _____

C | Match each Harf with its meaning.

A. However/But   1. لَعَلَّ

B. For sure/Indeed   2. إِنَّ

C. That   3. كَأَنَّ

D. So that, hopefully, maybe   4. لَيْتَ

E. As though   5. أَنَّ

F. If only   6. لَكِنَّ

D | Circle the Harf Nasb in each question.

1.
   A. فِي
   B. الَّذِينَ
   C. أَنَّ
   D. هُوَ

2.
   A. أَنْتَ
   B. الَّذِي
   C. إِلَى
   D. كَأَنَّ

3.
   A. عَلَى
   B. هُمْ
   C. إِنَّ
   D. هَذِهِ

4.
   A. اللَّاتِي
   B. أَنْتُمْ
   C. هَذَانِ
   D. لَكِنَّ

5.
   A. لَيْتَ
   B. الَّذِي
   C. أَنْتُنَّ
   D. جَنَّتَانِ

6.
   A. حُبَّ
   B. أَنَّ
   C. اللَّتَانِ
   D. هُنَّ

7.
   A. أَنَا
   B. لَعَلَّ
   C. اللَّذَانِ
   D. عَنْ

8.
   A. أَنَّهُمْ
   B. هُمْ
   C. مِنْ
   D. نَحْنُ

9.
   A. عَنْ
   B. لَكِنَّهَا
   C. هِيَ
   D. اللَّذَانِ

10.
    A. الَّذِينَ
    B. هُمَا
    C. اللَّتَانِ
    D. إِنَّكَ

11.
    A. أَنْتِ
    B. لَعَلَّهُ
    C. بِ
    D. تِلْكَ

12.
    A. حَتَّى
    B. هَذَانِ
    C. لَيْتَنِي
    D. أَنْتُمَا

Lesson 2

Accompanying Video
Unit 1: 1.9.2

Learning Goals • Practice identifying, translating, and labeling Harf Nasb fragments

A Watch the accompanying video. Based on what you hear and see in the video, write/circle the correct answer.

1. The job of the Harf Nasb is to make it's victim _____.

2. The _____ doesn't have to beat up the word that comes right after it, other words can come in between and then it's victim can come later in the sentence.

3. In لَكِنَّ أَكْثَرَ النَّاسِ, the اِسْمُ لَكِنَّ is _____.

4. In أَنَّ عَلَيْهِ النَّشْأَةَ, the اِسْمُ أَنَّ is _____.

5. In إِنَّ رَبَّكَ, the اِسْمُ إِنَّ is _____.

6. A Harf Nasb can only beat up a(n) _____.

7. فِي جَنَّاتٍ is a _____ fragment.

8. In أَنَّكُمْ, the اِسْمُ أَنَّ is _____.

9. In فِي أُذُنَيْهِ, the Majroor is _____.

10. In أَنَّ فِيكُمْ رَسُولَ اللَّهِ, the اِسْمُ أَنَّ is _____.

11. The translation of إِنَّ اللَّهَ is '_____'.

B | Fill in the blanks using the word bank.

> Can   Properties   Jarr   Ism   Nasb   Jobs   Can't   Victim

1. Isms have _____ and Harfs have _____.

2. The job of a Harf Jarr is to make the word after it _____.

3. The job of a Harf Nasb is to make the word after it _____.

4. You call the Harf Nasb what it is and the _____ of the Harf is called 'اِسْمُ + the Harf'. For example, for the fragment إِنَّ اَللَّهَ, you would say that the Harf Nasb إِنَّ and the word Allah is اِسْمُ إِنَّ.

5. A Harf Jarr and its victim _____ have a long distance relationship, but a Harf Nasb and its victim _____ have a long distance relationship. This means that a Harf Nasb and its victim don't have to be right next to each other.

6. The victim of a Harf Nasb has to be a(n) _____. So a Harf Jarr cannot be a victim because it is not an Ism.

C | **Circle the correct version of each fragment.**
Hint: Remember that the victim of a Harf Nasb must be in Nasb status.

1. A. إِنَّ اللَّهَ
   B. إِنَّ اللَّهُ
   C. إِنَّ اللَّهِ

2. A. لَيْتَنَحْنُ
   B. لَيْتَنَا
   C. لَيْتَهِيَ

3. A. أَنَّ بَيْتَيْنِ
   B. أَنَّ بَيْتَيْنَ
   C. أَنَّ بَيْتَانِ

4. A. إِنَّ مُؤْمِنٌ
   B. إِنَّ مُؤْمِنٍ
   C. إِنَّ مُؤْمِنًا

5. A. كَأَنَّ الغُرْفَةَ
   B. كَأَنَّ الغُرْفَةُ
   C. كَأَنَّ الغُرْفَةِ

6. A. لَكِنَّ الصَّالِحَاتِ
   B. لَكِنَّ الصَّالِحَاتُ
   C. لَكِنَّ الصَّالِحَاتَ

4. A. إِنَّهُوَ
   B. إِنَّأَنْتُمْ
   C. إِنَّكَ

8. A. لَعَلَّ الوَالِدِ
   B. لَعَلَّ الوَالِدَ
   C. لَعَلَّ الوَالِدُ

9. A. لَكِنَّ مَكَّةَ
   B. لَكِنَّ مَكَّةِ
   C. لَكِنَّ مَكَّةُ

10. A. لَيْتَنِي
    B. لَيْتَأَنَا
    C. لَيْتَأَنْتِ

11. A. لَعَلَّ فِرعَوْنٍ
    B. لَعَلَّ فِرعَوْنَ
    C. لَعَلَّ فِرعَوْنُ

12. A. لَكِنَّ الجَنَّتَيْنِ
    B. لَكِنَّ الجَنَّتَانِ
    C. لَكِنَّ الجَنَّتَانِ

D | Circle the Harf Nasb and underline its victim in each ayah.

1. أَوَلَا يَعْلَمُونَ أَنَّ اللَّهَ يَعْلَمُ مَا يُسِرُّونَ وَمَا يُعْلِنُونَ ﴿٧٧﴾

2. أَلَا إِنَّهُمْ هُمُ الْمُفْسِدُونَ وَلَٰكِن لَّا يَشْعُرُونَ ﴿١٢﴾

3. فَإِن زَلَلْتُم مِّن بَعْدِ مَا جَاءَتْكُمُ الْبَيِّنَاتُ فَاعْلَمُوا أَنَّ اللَّهَ عَزِيزٌ حَكِيمٌ ﴿٢٠٩﴾

4. .... وَإِنَّ فَرِيقًا مِّنْهُمْ لَيَكْتُمُونَ الْحَقَّ وَهُمْ يَعْلَمُونَ ﴿١٤٦﴾

5. ثُمَّ عَفَوْنَا عَنكُم مِّن بَعْدِ ذَٰلِكَ لَعَلَّكُمْ تَشْكُرُونَ ﴿٥٢﴾

6. إِنَّ اللَّهَ يُحِبُّ الَّذِينَ يُقَاتِلُونَ فِي سَبِيلِهِ صَفًّا كَأَنَّهُم بُنْيَانٌ مَّرْصُوصٌ ﴿٤﴾

7. وَالْعَصْرِ ﴿١﴾ إِنَّ الْإِنسَانَ لَفِي خُسْرٍ ﴿٢﴾

8. قِيلَ ادْخُلِ الْجَنَّةَ ۖ قَالَ يَا لَيْتَ قَوْمِي يَعْلَمُونَ ﴿٢٦﴾

9. فَسَبِّحْ بِحَمْدِ رَبِّكَ وَاسْتَغْفِرْهُ ۚ إِنَّهُ كَانَ تَوَّابًا ﴿٣﴾

10. وَلَوْ كَانُوا يُؤْمِنُونَ بِاللَّهِ وَالنَّبِيِّ وَمَا أُنزِلَ إِلَيْهِ مَا اتَّخَذُوهُمْ أَوْلِيَاءَ وَلَٰكِنَّ كَثِيرًا مِّنْهُمْ فَاسِقُونَ ﴿٨١﴾

E | Circle the Harf Nasb and underline its victim in each ayah. Then translate the Harf Nasb to complete the translation given.

1. __For sure/Indeed__ Allah is extremely forgiving and merciful — إِنَّ اللَّهَ غَفُورٌ رَّحِيمٌ

2. _____ the people of the cave — أَنَّ أَصْحَابَ الْكَهْفِ

3. _____ mankind is in a tremendous loss — إِنَّ الْإِنْسَانَ لَفِي خُسْرٍ

4. _____ in his ears is a barrier — كَأَنَّ فِي أُذُنَيْهِ وَقْرًا

5. _____ I had done good in my life! — يَا لَيْتَنِي قَدَّمْتُ لِحَيَاتِي

6. _____ Allah guides whoever He wishes — وَلَٰكِنَّ اللَّهَ يَهْدِي مَن يَشَاءُ

7. _____ _____ obtain mercy — لَعَلَّكُمْ تُرْحَمُونَ

8. He said, "_____ my people could know!" — قَالَ يَا لَيْتَ قَوْمِي يَعْلَمُونَ

9. _____ He is ever accepting of repentance — إِنَّهُ كَانَ تَوَّابًا

10. _____ Allah reconciled between them — وَلَٰكِنَّ اللَّهَ أَلَّفَ بَيْنَهُمْ

Bayyinah Institute • Chapter 4

F | **Translate the following fragments into Arabic using the word bank.**

House	بَيْتٌ	Door	بَابٌ	Messenger	رَسُولٌ
Pen	قَلَمٌ	Room	غُرْفَةٌ	Teacher	مُعَلِّمٌ
Allah	اَللَّهُ	Book	كِتَابٌ	Friend	صَدِيقٌ

1. That the book _____

2. Indeed, Allah _____

3. If only she _____

4. That the Messenger of Allah _____

5. Maybe the pen _____

6. However, their room _____

7. Indeed, my friend _____

8. However, his teacher _____

Lesson 3

Learning Goals • Memorize the special Mudhaafs with their meanings

Accompanying Video
Unit 1: 1.10.1

A | Watch the accompanying video. Based on what you hear and see in the video, write/circle the correct answer.

1. فَوْقَ means '_____'.

2. تَحْتَ means '_____'.

3. قَبْلَ means '_____'.

4. بَعْدَ means '_____'.

5. خَلْفَ means '_____'.

6. بَيْنَ means '_____'.

7. حَوْلَ means '_____'.

8. مَعَ means '_____'.

9. كُلُّ means '_____'.
   A. 'All of'   B. 'Above'   C. 'Behind'

10. بَعْضُكُمْ means '_____'.

11. أَيُّهُمْ means '_____'.

12. دُونَ ذَلِكَ means '_____'.

13. عِنْدَكَ means '_____'.

Bayyinah Institute • Chapter 4

B | Fill in the blanks using the word bank.

> Many   Doesn't   Mudhaaf Ilayh   Idhaafah   Mudhaaf
> وَرَاءَ   تَحْتَ   خَلْفَ   غَيْرَهَا   فَوْقَ

1. A(n) _____ is a fragment that usually means '___ of ___'.

2. Special Mudhaafs are special because they make an Idhaafah that _____ mean '___ of ___'.

3. A special Mudhaaf is a _____ and the word after it is a _____.

4. There are _____ special Mudhaafs in the Qur'an.

5. _____ means 'below' and _____ means 'above'.

6. _____ and _____ both mean 'behind'.

7. _____ means 'without her'.

C

Match each word with its meaning. They have been divided up so that 1-5 match with A-E, 6-10 match with F-J, and 11-15 match with K-O.

A. Below	1. قَبْلَ
B. After	2. تَحْتَ
C. Before	3. خَلْفَ/وَرَاءَ
D. Above	4. فَوْقَ
E. Behind	5. بَعْدَ
F. Around	6. غَيْرَ
G. Between	7. عِنْدَ
H. Besides, other than	8. حَوْلَ
I. Without/Non	9. بَيْنَ
J. Has, with, nearby	10. دُونَ
K. Which	11. كُلَّ
L. Especially from	12. مَعَ
M. With	13. أَيُّ
N. All of	14. بَعْضُ
O. Some of	15. لَدُنْ

BUILDING VOCABULARY

D | Circle the special Mudhaaf in each question.

1. A. هَذَا
   B. الَّذِينَ
   C. فَوْقَ
   D. هُوَ

2. A. أَنْتَ
   B. الَّذِي
   C. أَنَّ
   D. قَبْلَ

3. A. اللَّتَانِ
   B. هُمْ
   C. تَحْتَ
   D. هَذِهِ

4. A. إِنَّ
   B. أَنْتُمْ
   C. هَذَانِ
   D. خَلْفَ

5. A. بَعْدَ
   B. الَّذِي
   C. أَنْتُنَّ
   D. فِي

6. A. كَأَنَّ
   B. غَيْرَ
   C. عَنْ
   D. هُنَّ

7. A. أَنَا
   B. عِنْدَ
   C. اللَّذَانِ
   D. عَلَى

8. A. حَوْلَ
   B. هُمْ
   C. إِلَى
   D. نَحْنُ

9. A. اللَّتَانِ
   B. لَيْتَ
   C. هِيَ
   D. بَيْنَ

10. A. ذَلِكَ
    B. هُمَا
    C. اللَّتَانِ
    D. دُونَ

11. A. أَنْتِ
    B. لَكِنَّ
    C. بَعْضَ
    D. تِلْكَ

12. A. حَتَّى
    B. أَيُّ
    C. لَعَلَّ
    D. أَنْتُمَا

E | Translate the underlined word in each of the following questions into Arabic.

Date: _____

1. The pen fell <u>behind</u> the desk. _____

2. The boys ran <u>around</u> the car. _____

3. She hid <u>underneath</u> the table. _____

4. The city is <u>between</u> two rivers. _____

5. <u>Some of</u> the students failed. _____

6. <u>All of</u> the girls woke up on time. _____

7. They studied <u>before</u> school. _____

8. <u>Which</u> fruit do you like best? _____

9. She went <u>with</u> her mom. _____

10. He found it <u>above</u> the fridge. _____

BUILDING VOCABULARY

F | Circle the correct version of each fragment.
Hint: Remember that a word after a special Mudhaaf has to be in Jarr status.

1. A. حَوْلَ بَيْتٌ
   B. حَوْلَ بَيْتاً
   C. حَوْلَ بَيْتٍ

2. A. مَعَ الكِتابِ
   B. مَعَ الكِتابُ
   C. مَعَ الكِتابَ

3. A. تَحْتَ طَاوِلَةٌ
   B. تَحْتَ طَاوِلَةٍ
   C. تَحْتَ طَاوِلَةً

4. A. لَدُنْهُ
   B. لَدُنْهَ
   C. لَدُنْهِ

5. A. خَلْفَ الغُرْفَةَ
   B. خَلْفَ الغُرْفَةُ
   C. خَلْفَ الغُرْفَةِ

6. A. مَعَهُمْ
   B. مَعَهِمْ
   C. مَعَهَمْ

7. A. بَعْضَ الطُّلَّابِ
   B. بَعْضَ الطُّلَّابِ
   C. بَعْضَ الطُّلَّابُ

8. A. غَيْرَ كُمْ
   B. غَيْرَ كَمْ
   C. غَيْرَ كِمْ

9. A. كُلُّ المُسْلِمِينِ
   B. كُلُّ المُسْلِمُونَ
   C. كُلُّ المُسْلِمِينَ

10. A. بَعْدَ مُوسَى
    B. بَعْدَ مُوسَيْ
    C. بَعْدَ مُوسِي

11. A. بَيْنَ وَلَدَانِ
    B. بَيْنَ وَلَدَيْنِ
    C. بَيْنَ وَلَدَيْنَ

12. A. عِنْدَيْ
    B. عِنْدِي
    C. عِنْدِيَ

G | Translate the following fragments into Arabic using the word bank.

House	بَيْتٌ	Door	بَابٌ	Messenger	رَسُولٌ
Pen	قَلَمٌ	Room	غُرْفَةٌ	Teacher	مُعَلِّمٌ
Allah	اَللَّهُ	Book	كِتَابٌ	Friend	صَدِيقٌ

1. Around the house

2. Behind the door

3. With the teacher

4. Between two friends

5. Without a pen

6. Beside my house

7. Above my friend's book

8. Some of our teachers (مُعَلِّمُونَ)

BUILDING VOCABULARY

H | Find all of the special Mudhaafs in the ayahs below, then translate each of the special Mudhaafs.

1. وَهُوَ الْقَاهِرُ فَوْقَ عِبَادِهِ ۚ وَهُوَ الْحَكِيمُ الْخَبِيرُ ﴿١٨﴾
   _____

2. أَعَدَّ اللَّهُ لَهُمْ جَنَّاتٍ تَجْرِي مِن تَحْتِهَا الْأَنْهَارُ خَالِدِينَ فِيهَا ۚ ذَٰلِكَ الْفَوْزُ الْعَظِيمُ ﴿٨٩﴾
   _____

3. وَالَّذِينَ يُؤْمِنُونَ بِمَا أُنزِلَ إِلَيْكَ وَمَا أُنزِلَ مِن قَبْلِكَ وَبِالْآخِرَةِ هُمْ يُوقِنُونَ ﴿٤﴾
   _____

4. ثُمَّ عَفَوْنَا عَنكُم مِّن بَعْدِ ذَٰلِكَ لَعَلَّكُمْ تَشْكُرُونَ ﴿٥٢﴾
   _____

5. لَهُم مِّن جَهَنَّمَ مِهَادٌ وَمِن فَوْقِهِمْ غَوَاشٍ ۚ وَكَذَٰلِكَ نَجْزِي الظَّالِمِينَ ﴿٤١﴾
   _____

6. نَزَّلَ عَلَيْكَ الْكِتَابَ بِالْحَقِّ مُصَدِّقًا لِّمَا بَيْنَ يَدَيْهِ وَأَنزَلَ التَّوْرَاةَ وَالْإِنجِيلَ ﴿٣﴾
   _____

7. وَلَقَدْ كُنتُمْ تَمَنَّوْنَ الْمَوْتَ مِن قَبْلِ أَن تَلْقَوْهُ فَقَدْ رَأَيْتُمُوهُ وَأَنتُمْ تَنظُرُونَ ﴿١٤٣﴾
   _____

8. ثُمَّ بَعَثْنَاهُمْ لِنَعْلَمَ أَيُّ الْحِزْبَيْنِ أَحْصَىٰ لِمَا لَبِثُوا أَمَدًا ﴿١٢﴾
   _____

9. وَلَوْ جَاءَتْهُمْ كُلُّ آيَةٍ حَتَّىٰ يَرَوُا الْعَذَابَ الْأَلِيمَ ﴿٩٧﴾
   _____

10. هُمْ دَرَجَاتٌ عِندَ اللَّهِ ۗ وَاللَّهُ بَصِيرٌ بِمَا يَعْمَلُونَ ﴿١٦٣﴾
    _____

Date: _____

Determine if each fragment is an Idhaafah. If it is, write the Mudhaaf and Mudhaaf Ilayh. If it isn't, write which fragment it is.

Mudhaaf Ilayh	Mudhaaf			
هُمْ	أَيُّ	Yes	No	1. أَيُّهُمْ
		Yes	No	2. إِلَى البَيْتِ
		Yes	No	3. وَالتِّينِ
		Yes	No	4. بَعْضُهُمْ
		Yes	No	5. إِنَّ الإِنْسَانَ
		Yes	No	6. بِالحَقِّ
		Yes	No	7. وَرَآئِهِمْ
		Yes	No	8. كَأَنَّكَ
		Yes	No	9. دُونَ ذَلِكَ
		Yes	No	10. بَيْنَ الأُخْتَيْنِ

Bayyinah Institute • Chapter 4

Qur'anic Application

Circle all the Harf Nasb below.

تَبَارَكَ الَّذِي بِيَدِهِ الْمُلْكُ وَهُوَ عَلَىٰ كُلِّ شَيْءٍ قَدِيرٌ ۝ الَّذِي خَلَقَ الْمَوْتَ وَالْحَيَاةَ لِيَبْلُوَكُمْ أَيُّكُمْ أَحْسَنُ عَمَلًا ۚ وَهُوَ الْعَزِيزُ الْغَفُورُ ۝ الَّذِي خَلَقَ سَبْعَ سَمَاوَاتٍ طِبَاقًا ۖ مَّا تَرَىٰ فِي خَلْقِ الرَّحْمَٰنِ مِن تَفَاوُتٍ ۖ فَارْجِعِ الْبَصَرَ هَلْ تَرَىٰ مِن فُطُورٍ ۝ ثُمَّ ارْجِعِ الْبَصَرَ كَرَّتَيْنِ يَنقَلِبْ إِلَيْكَ الْبَصَرُ خَاسِئًا وَهُوَ حَسِيرٌ ۝ وَلَقَدْ زَيَّنَّا السَّمَاءَ الدُّنْيَا بِمَصَابِيحَ وَجَعَلْنَاهَا رُجُومًا لِّلشَّيَاطِينِ ۖ وَأَعْتَدْنَا لَهُمْ عَذَابَ السَّعِيرِ ۝ وَلِلَّذِينَ كَفَرُوا بِرَبِّهِمْ عَذَابُ جَهَنَّمَ ۖ وَبِئْسَ الْمَصِيرُ ۝

CHAPTER 5
Mawsoof Sifah

Chapter 5

The Mawsoof Sifah الْمَوْصُوْفُ وَ الصِّفَةُ fragment is analogous to nouns and adjectives. The fragment is comprised of two parts:

1) **Mawsoof:** This is the "noun" and it has to be an Ism.

2) **Sifah:** This is the "adjective" and it can be one or more Isms.

Example

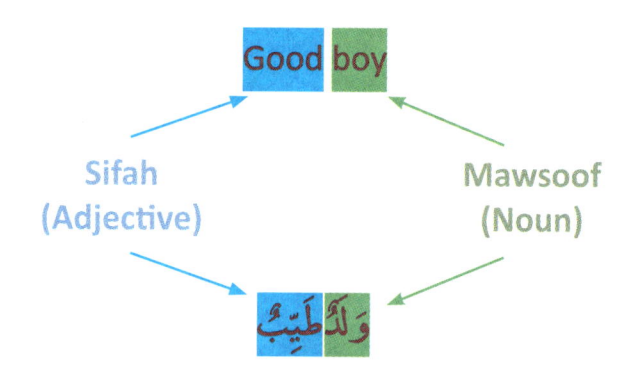

Good boy

Sifah (Adjective)   Mawsoof (Noun)

وَلَدٌ طَيِّبٌ

Notice a few key points:

1) In Arabic, the noun (Mawsoof) comes first, the adjective (Sifah) comes second.

2) All four properties of the Mawsoof and Sifah match.

3) You can have more than one Sifah, e.g. وَلَدٌ طَيِّبٌ طَوِيلٌ Good, tall boy.

Rules for Mawsoof Sifah

1) All four properties of the Mawsoof and Sifah must match.

Application

Are the following Mawsoof Sifah fragments?

مُسْلِمَةٌ صَالِحَةٌ

✓ All four properties match (Raf', Singular, Feminine, Common)

Translation: A righteous Muslim girl

✓ **Mawsoof Sifah**

المُسْلِمَانِ الصَّالِحَانِ

✓ Mawsoof Sifah

✓ All four properties match (Raf', Pair, Masculine, Proper)

Translation: Two righteous Muslims

وَإِنَّ الدَّارَ الْآخِرَةَ لَهِيَ الْحَيَوَانُ

✓ Mawsoof Sifah

✓ All four properties match (Nasb, Singular, Feminine, Proper)

Translation: The later home (i.e. the home in the afterlife)

وَلَدَارُ الْآخِرَةِ خَيْرٌ لِّلَّذِينَ اتَّقَوْا

✗ Mawsoof Sifah

✗ دَارُ is Raf', الْآخِرَةِ is Jarr

Translation: The home of the later life

فِيهَا كُتُبٌ قَيِّمَةٌ

✓ Mawsoof Sifah

✓ كُتُبٌ is Raf; قَيِّمَةٌ is Raf.

✓ كُتُبٌ is a broken plural, so it is singular and feminine.

✓ قَيِّمَةٌ is singular and feminine.

✓ كُتُبٌ is common; قَيِّمَةٌ is common.

Translation: Upright books.

Multiple Fragments

Consider the following:

حَيَاتُنَا الدُّنْيَا

What fragment is حَيَاتُنَا؟

- حَيَاتُ is light, no ال, followed by attached pronoun نَا (Jarr) so it is Mudhaaf and Mudhaaf Ilayh.
- Another way of looking at this: نَا is attached to an Ism so it is Mudhaaf and Mudhaaf Ilayh.

What are the properties of الدُّنْيَا؟

- Status could be Raf/Nasb/Jarr. Number is singular. Gender is feminine. Type is proper.

What are the properties of حَيَاتُ؟

- Status is Raf. Number is singular. Gender is feminine. Type is proper because it is Mudhaaf to نَا which is always proper.

The four properties match, so حَيَاتُ and الدُّنْيَا are actually Mawsoof Sifah. We have two fragments here: Idhaafah and Mawsoof Sifah.

Idhaafah
حَيَاتُنَا الدُّنْيَا
Mawsoof Sifah

Translation: Our worldly life.

Lesson 1

Accompanying Video
Unit 1: 1.11.1

Learning Goals • Identifying Mawsoof Sifah fragments • Identify Mawsoof and Sifah

A | Watch the accompanying video. Based on what you hear and see in the video, write/circle the correct answer.

1. In English, when an adjective describes a noun, the adjective always comes before the noun, but in Arabic, the adjective always comes _____ the noun.

2. In Arabic, the thing being described (the noun) is called the _____, the description (adjective) is called the _____.
   A. Sifah/Mawsoof   B. Mawsoof/Sifah   C. Majroor/Sifah

3. In the fragment 'beautiful cars', '_____' is the Sifah.

4. In a Mawsoof and Sifah fragment, the Mawsoof and Sifah must match in all four _____.

5. _____ is the correct Sifah for المُسْلِمِينَ.
   A. صَالِحِينَ   B. صَالِحَيْنِ   C. الصَّالِحُونَ   D. الصَّالِحِينَ

6. For all non-human plurals (whether feminine or broken), their Sifah must be singular and feminine. So the correct Sifah for بُيُوتٌ (houses) would be _____.

Bayyinah Institute • Chapter 5

B | Fill in the blanks using the word bank.

> Four   After   Common   First   Sifah   Five   Raf'
> Idhaafah   Singular   Mawsoof   Masculine

1. There are _____ fragments in Arabic. You have learned three of them so far: _____, Harf Jarr, and Harf Nasb. The fourth fragment is called Mawsoof Sifah.

2. _____ is the word being described and the _____ is the adjective.

3. In English, the Sifah goes _____. However, in Arabic, the Sifah comes _____ the Mawsoof.

4. The _____ properties of the Mawsoof have to match the four properties of the Sifah.

5. In the fragment مُسْلِمٌ صَالِحٌ, the four properties of مُسْلِمٌ are _____, singular, _____, and common. The four properties of صَالِحٌ are Raf', _____, masculine, and _____. Since the two words have the same properties, the words make a Mawsoof Sifah.

Chapter 5 • Bayyinah Institute

C | **Circle the Mawsoof Sifah fragment in each question.**

Date: _____

1.
   A. This book
   B. A book
   C. New book
   D. With the book

2.
   A. The boys
   B. Good boy
   C. A boy
   D. All the boys

3.
   A. That school
   B. Our school
   C. The big school
   D. In the school

4.
   A. All of those girls
   B. Tall girls
   C. The girls
   D. The girls' team

5.
   A. That phone
   B. My phone
   C. A phone
   D. Two old phones

6.
   A. Like my plates
   B. With the plates
   C. Underneath the plate
   D. Pretty plates

7.
   A. The computer
   B. Fast computers
   C. Those computers
   D. My computer

8.
   A. My house
   B. That house
   C. Big houses
   D. All the houses

9.
   A. Under the desk
   B. The wide desk
   C. On the desk
   D. Her desk

10.
    A. Tall trees
    B. Under the tree
    C. At the tree
    D. All the trees

11.
    A. Those kids
    B. Smart kids
    C. My kids
    D. Their teacher

12.
    A. The pretty card
    B. A card
    C. This card
    D. On the card

Bayyinah Institute • Chapter 5

D — Determine if each fragment is a Mawsoof Sifah. If it is, circle the Mawsoof and underline the Sifah. If not, leave it as is.

1. My cat
2. Allah's house
3. Giant mansion — (Mawsoof: mansion; Sifah: Giant)
4. The building's height
5. Hard lesson — (Mawsoof: lesson; Sifah: Hard)
6. Our pets
7. Tall plants — (Mawsoof: plants; Sifah: Tall)
8. New desk — (Mawsoof: desk; Sifah: New)
9. Fast cars — (Mawsoof: cars; Sifah: Fast)
10. This building
11. The clear water — (Mawsoof: water; Sifah: clear)
12. Night of Power
13. Big glass — (Mawsoof: glass; Sifah: Big)
14. Hijab of a girl
15. Messenger of Allah
16. Your house
17. Beautiful art — (Mawsoof: art; Sifah: Beautiful)
18. Creator of the universe
19. Comfortable couch — (Mawsoof: couch; Sifah: Comfortable)
20. Healthy children — (Mawsoof: children; Sifah: Healthy)
21. Their happiness
22. The sturdy chair — (Mawsoof: chair; Sifah: sturdy)
23. The queen's palace
24. People of the Book
25. Smart girl — (Mawsoof: girl; Sifah: Smart)
26. The expensive car — (Mawsoof: car; Sifah: expensive)
27. Our signs
28. New books — (Mawsoof: books; Sifah: New)
29. The country's safety
30. Their hands

Date: _____

E | Write the four properties of each of the following words and determine if they are a Mawsoof Sifah.

1. بَابٌ جَدِيدٌ

Can it be a Mawsoof Sifah?   Yes   No

بَابٌ

_____ _____ _____ _____
(Status)   (Number)   (Gender)   (Type)

جَدِيدٌ

_____ _____ _____ _____
(Status)   (Number)   (Gender)   (Type)

2. مُؤْمِنَةٌ صَالِحَةٌ

Can it be a Mawsoof Sifah?   Yes   No

مُؤْمِنَةٌ

_____ _____ _____ _____
(Status)   (Number)   (Gender)   (Type)

صَالِحَةٌ

_____ _____ _____ _____
(Status)   (Number)   (Gender)   (Type)

3. بَيْتَانِ كَبِيرَةٌ

Can it be a Mawsoof Sifah?   Yes   No

بَيْتَانِ

_____ _____ _____ _____
(Status)   (Number)   (Gender)   (Type)

كَبِيرَةٌ

_____ _____ _____ _____
(Status)   (Number)   (Gender)   (Type)

Date: _____

4. رِحْلَةَ الشِّتَاءِ   Can it be a Mawsoof Sifah?   Yes   No

رِحْلَةَ
_____   _____   _____   _____
(Status)   (Number)   (Gender)   (Type)

الشِّتَاءِ
_____   _____   _____   _____
(Status)   (Number)   (Gender)   (Type)

5. نَاراً حَامِيَةً   Can it be a Mawsoof Sifah?   Yes   No

نَاراً
_____   _____   _____   _____
(Status)   (Number)   (Gender)   (Type)

حَامِيَةً
_____   _____   _____   _____
(Status)   (Number)   (Gender)   (Type)

6. نَذِيرٌ مُّبِينٌ   Can it be a Mawsoof Sifah?   Yes   No

نَذِيرٌ
_____   _____   _____   _____
(Status)   (Number)   (Gender)   (Type)

مُّبِينٌ
_____   _____   _____   _____
(Status)   (Number)   (Gender)   (Type)

F | Translate the following fragments into Arabic using the word bank.
Hint: Remember that 'the' implies that the word is proper.

House	بَيْتٌ	Room	غُرْفَةٌ	New	جَدِيدٌ
Friend	صَدِيقٍ	Book	كِتَابٌ	Good	صَالِحٌ
Teacher	مُعَلِّمٌ	Small	صَغِيرٌ	Big	كَبِيرٌ

1. The big house

2. A good friend

3. A new teacher (f)

4. Two small books

5. A small house

6. The two new teachers (f)

7. Two good Muslims

8. Two small rooms

G | Determine if each fragment is a Mawsoof Sifah. If it is, circle the Mawsoof and underline the Sifah. If not, leave it as is.

1. مُسْلِمَةٌ ذَكِيَّةٌ
2. نَاراً حَامِيَةً
3. السَّمَاوَاتِ وَ الأَرْضِ
4. قَوْمُ لُوطٍ
5. بَيْنِ الصُّلْبِ
6. يَوْمَ الحَجِّ
7. أَوَّلُ المُسْلِمِينَ
8. أَحْسَنُ دِيناً
9. نَذِيرٌ مُبِينٌ
10. جَنَّاتُ عَدْنٍ

11. عَيْنَانِ نَضَّاخَتَانِ
12. الصِّرَاطَ المُسْتَقِيمَ
13. يَوْمَ الحَجِّ
14. أَمَداً بَعِيداً
15. قَرْناً آخَرِينَ
16. رَبُّ السَّمَاوَاتِ
17. عَذَابٌ أَلِيمٌ
18. مَلِكِ النَّاسِ
19. لَيْلَةِ القَدْرِ
20. جَنَّتَانِ مُدْهَامَّتَانِ

21. ثَمَناً قَلِيلاً
22. المَسْجِدِ الحَرَامِ
23. رِحْلَةَ الشِّتَاءِ
24. أَجْراً عَظِيماً
25. شَرِّ الوَسْوَاسِ
26. طَعَامِ المِسْكِينِ
27. عَصْفٍ مَأْكُولٍ
28. أَهْلَ الكِتَابِ
29. القَوْمَ الفَاسِقِينَ
30. بَنِي إِسْرَائِيلَ

Lesson 2

Accompanying Video
Unit 1: 1.11.2

Learning Goals • Practice identifying and writing Mawsoof Sifah fragments

A Watch the accompanying video. Based on what you hear and see in the video, write/circle the correct answer.

1. In English, the Mawsoof goes _____. In Arabic, the Mawsoof goes first.

2. يَوْمِ القِيَامَةِ is a _____ fragment.
   A. Mudhaaf and Mudhaaf Ilayh   B. Harf Jarr   C. Harf Nasb   D. Mawsoof Sifah

3. الفَوْزُ المُبِينُ is a _____ fragment.
   A. Mudhaaf and Mudhaaf Ilayh   B. Harf Jarr   C. Harf Nasb   D. Mawsoof Sifah

4. أَسَاطِيرُ الأَوَّلِينَ is a _____ fragment.
   A. Mudhaaf and Mudhaaf Ilayh   B. Harf Jarr   C. Harf Nasb   D. Mawsoof Sifah

5. If the Mudhaaf Ilayh is proper, then the _____ is proper (if the word after 'of' is proper, then the word before 'of' is proper).

6. Between a Mawsoof and a Sifah you can have other _____, the Mawsoof and Sifah don't always have to be right next to each other.

7. الحَيَاةُ الدُّنْيَا is a _____ fragment.
   A. Mudhaaf and Mudhaaf Ilayh   B. Harf Jarr   C. Harf Nasb   D. Mawsoof Sifah

8. إِنَّ اللَّهَ is a _____ fragment.
   A. Mudhaaf and Mudhaaf Ilayh   B. Harf Jarr   C. Harf Nasb   D. Mawsoof Sifah

B | Fill in the blanks using the word bank.

> After   Common   Feminine   Fragment   Plural   Properties
> Mawsoof Sifah   Sifah   Mawsoof   Before   Raf'   Next

1. The fourth _____ we're learning is Mawsoof Sifah.

2. _____ is the word being described and the _____ is the adjective.

3. In English, the Sifah comes _____ the Mawsoof. But in Arabic, the Sifah comes _____ the Mawsoof.

4. The four _____ of the Mawsoof and Sifah have to be the same.

5. In the fragment مُسْلِمَاتٌ صَالِحَاتٌ, the four properties of مُسْلِمَاتٌ are _____, plural, _____, and common. The four properties of صَالِحَاتٌ are Raf', _____, feminine, and _____. Since the two words have the same properties, the words make a _____.

6. Mawsoof and Sifah don't have to be _____ to each other, they can have a long distance relationship.

C. Determine if each fragment can be a Mawsoof Sifah. If it can, translate using the word bank. If not, write why not.

Word Bank:
House بَيْتٌ	City مَدِينَةٌ	New جَدِيدٌ
Houses بُيُوتٌ	Cities مُدُنٌ	Good صَالِحٌ
Visitor زَائِرٌ	Teacher مُعَلِّمٌ	Big كَبِيرٌ

1. مَدِينَةٌ كَبِيرَةٌ — A big city

2. مَدِينَتَيْنِ كَبِيرَةً — Not a Mawsoof Sifah (number/case mismatch)

3. مُدُنٍ كَبِيرَاتٌ — Not a Mawsoof Sifah (case mismatch)

4. الْمَدِينَةَ الْكَبِيرَةَ — The big city

5. الْمَدِينَتَانِ الْكَبِيرَتَانِ — The two big cities

6. الْمُدُنِ الْكَبِيرَةِ — The big cities

7. بَيْتاً جَدِيداً — A new house

8. بَيْتَانِ جَدِيدَتَانِ — Not a Mawsoof Sifah (gender mismatch)

9. بُيُوتٍ جَدِيدَةٍ — New houses

10. الْبَيْتُ جَدِيدٌ — Not a Mawsoof Sifah (definiteness mismatch — this is a sentence)

18. المُسَاعِدَاتُ الصَّالِحَاتُ	11. البَيْتَيْنِ الجَدِيدَيْنِ
19. زَائِراً جَدِيداً	12. البُيُوتُ الجَدِيدُ
20. زَائِرِينَ جَدِيدَةٍ	13. مُسَاعِدَةٌ صَالِحَةٌ
21. زَائِرَيْنِ جَدِيدَتَيْنِ	14. مُسَاعِدَتَيْنِ صَالِحَةٍ
22. الزَّائِرُ الجَدِيدُ	15. مُسَاعِدَاتٍ صَالِحَاتٍ
23. الزَّائِرَانِ الجَدِيدَانِ	16. المُسَاعِدَةُ الصَّالِحَةُ
24. الزَّائِرُونَ الجُدُدُ (Plural of جَدِيدٌ)	17. المُسَاعِدَتَانِ الصَّالِحَانِ

Date: _____

D | Translate the following fragments into Arabic using the word bank.

House	بَيْتٌ	Book	كِتَابٌ	New	جَدِيدٌ
Houses	بُيُوتٌ	Books	كُتُبٌ	Good	صَالِحٌ
Teacher	مُعَلِّمٌ	Worker	عَامِلٌ	Big	كَبِيرٌ

1. A big house

2. Two big houses

3. Big houses

4. The big house

5. The two big houses

6. The big houses

7. A new book

8. Two new books

9. New books

10. The new book

BUILDING VOCABULARY

Date: _____

11. The two new books

_____

12. The new books

_____

13. A good teacher

_____

14. Two good teachers

_____

15. Good teachers

_____

16. The good teacher

_____

17. The two good teachers

_____

18. The good teachers

_____

19. A new female worker

_____

20. Two new female workers

_____

21. New female workers

_____

22. The new female worker

_____

23. The two new female workers

_____

24. The new female workers

_____

E — Label each of the following fragments.
Hint: It can be an Idhaafah, Harf Jarr, Harf Nasb, or Mawsoof Sifah.

1. إِنَّ اللَّهَ

2. رَبِّ العَالَمِينَ

3. عَيْنٌ جَارِيَةٌ

4. عِيشَةٍ رَاضِيَةٍ

5. حُبِّ الخَيْرِ

6. الفَوْزُ المُبِينُ

7. الحَيَاةُ الدُّنْيَا

8. إِلَى السَّمَاءِ

9. إِنَّكَ

10. كُلِّ شَيْءٍ

11. يَوْمٍ عَظِيمٍ

12. أَسَاطِيرُ الأَوَّلِينَ

Lesson 3

Accompanying Video
Unit 1: 1.11.3

Learning Goals • Practice identifying Mawsoof Sifah fragments

A | Watch the accompanying video. Based on what you hear and see in the video, write/circle the correct answer.

1. اَلْقَوْمُ الظَّالِمُونَ is a _____ fragment.

   A. Mudhaaf and Mudhaaf Ilayh   B. Harf Jarr   C. Harf Nasb   D. Mawsoof Sifah

2. عَيْنٌ is _____ in gender because it is a body part that occurs in pairs.

3. كَالْفَرَاشِ is a _____ fragment.

   A. Mudhaaf and Mudhaaf Ilayh   B. Harf Jarr   C. Harf Nasb   D. Mawsoof Sifah

4. عِيشَةٍ رَاضِيَةٍ is a _____ fragment.

   A. Mudhaaf and Mudhaaf Ilayh   B. Harf Jarr   C. Harf Nasb   D. Mawsoof Sifah

5. وَالْعَادِيَاتِ is a _____ fragment.

   A. Mudhaaf and Mudhaaf Ilayh   B. Harf Jarr   C. Harf Nasb   D. Mawsoof Sifah

6. نَارٌ is _____ in gender because the Arabs said so.

7. الْعِهْنِ الْمَنْفُوشِ is a _____ fragment.

   A. Mudhaaf and Mudhaaf Ilayh   B. Harf Jarr   C. Harf Nasb   D. Mawsoof Sifah

8. In the fragment كُتُبٌ قَيِّمَةٌ, the word كُتُبٌ is plural in meaning but is grammatically treated as _____.

Bayyinah Institute • Chapter 5

B | Determine if each fragment is a Mawsoof Sifah. If it is, circle the Mawsoof and underline the Sifah. If not, leave it as is.

1. قَوْلًا ثَقِيلًا
2. الْمَسْجِدِ الْحَرَامِ
3. كَلَامَ اللَّهِ
4. عَيْنٌ جَارِيَةٌ
5. أَجْراً عَظِيماً
6. شَرِّ الْوَسْوَاسِ
7. طَعَامِ الْمِسْكِينِ
8. عَصْفٍ مَأْكُولٍ
9. كَالْعِهْنِ الْمَنْفُوشِ
10. الْقَوْمَ الْفَاسِقِينَ

11. مُسْلِمَةٌ ذَكِيَّةٌ
12. نَاراً حَامِيَةً
13. كَالْفَرَاشِ الْمَبْثُوثِ
14. قَوْمُ لُوطٍ
15. سَبْحاً طَوِيلاً
16. كُتُبٌ قَيِّمَةٌ
17. أَوَّلُ الْمُسْلِمِينَ
18. إِنَّ اللَّهَ قَادِرٌ
19. نَذِيرٌ مُبِينٌ
20. أَهْلُ الْكِتَابِ

21. عَيْنَانِ نَضَّاخَتَانِ
22. الصِّرَاطَ الْمُسْتَقِيمَ
23. يَوْمَ الْحَجِّ
24. الْقَوْمُ الظَّالِمُونَ
25. قَرْناً آخَرِينَ
26. رَبُّ السَّمَاوَاتِ
27. عَذَابٌ أَلِيمٌ
28. سِحْرٌ مُبِينٌ
29. صَيْحَةً وَاحِدَةً
30. عِيشَةٍ رَاضِيَةٍ

C | Label each of the following fragments.
Hint: It can be an Idhaafah, Harf Jarr, Harf Nasb, or Mawsoof Sifah.

1. كَثِيبًا مَهِيلًا

2. إِنَّكُمْ

3. كَالْفَرَاشِ

4. مِثْقَالَ ذَرَّةٍ

5. كُتُبٌ قَيِّمَةٌ

6. الْمُسَاعَدَةَ الصَّالِحَةَ

7. الْحَيَاةُ الدُّنْيَا

8. الْعِهْنِ الْمَنْفُوشِ

9. نَارٌ حَامِيَةٌ

10. كُلِّ شَيْءٍ

11. الْقَوْمُ الظَّالِمُونَ

12. مِنَ الشَّيْطَانِ

Bayyinah Institute • Chapter 5

D | Each of the phrases below has two or more fragments attached together. Label each part of the fragment.

1. عَلَى طَاوِلَتِهِ الْكَبِيرَةِ
   - Jaar / Majroor / Mudhaaf / Mudhaaf ilayh / Mawsoof / Sifah

2. بُيُوتُكَ الْجَدِيدَةُ

3. إِلَى مَدِينَةٍ جَدِيدَةٍ

4. مَعَ مُسَاعِدَةٍ صَالِحَةٍ

5. بَيْتُهَا الْبَارِدُ

6. بَيْنَ الْكِتَابَيْنِ الْجَدِيدَيْنِ

7. فِي مَدْرَسَةٍ كَبِيرَةٍ

8. عَنْ مُعَلِّمِيكَ الصَّالِحِينَ

9. حَتَّى مَطْلَعِ الْفَجْرِ

10. لِلْمُعَلِّمَاتِ الصَّالِحَاتِ

E. Translate the following fragments into Arabic using the word bank.

House	بَيْتٌ	Book	كِتَابٌ	City	مَدِينَةٌ
Houses	بُيُوتٌ	Books	كُتُبٌ	Cities	مُدُنٌ
New	جَدِيدٌ	Wide	وَاسِعٌ	Big	كَبِيرٌ

1. A wide house

2. Two wide houses

3. Wide houses

4. The wide house

5. The two wide houses

6. The wide houses

7. A new city

8. Two new cities

9. New cities

10. The new city

Date: _____

11. The two new cities

12. The new cities

13. A big book

14. Two big books

15. Big books

16. The big book

17. The two big books

18. The big books

19. A new house

20. Two new houses

21. New houses

22. The new house

23. The two new houses

24. The new houses

Lesson 4

Accompanying Video
Unit 1: 1.11.4

Learning Goals • Practice identifying and writing Mawsoof Sifah fragments

A
Watch the accompanying video. Based on what you hear and see in the video, write/circle the correct answer.

1. سَرِيرٌ is _____ in gender.

2. سُرُرٌ is _____ in gender because it is a non-human broken plural.

3. الجَبَلَيْنِ الكَبِيرَانِ match in every property except _____.

4. الجِبَالُ الكَبِيرُ match in every property except _____.

5. A human broken plural can be treated as _____ or as what it really is.

6. الكُتُبُ قَيِّمَةٌ match in every property except _____.

7. The number of both المُدُنِ and الجَمِيلَةِ is _____.

8. To know whether a Mudhaaf is proper or common, you have to look at the _____.

9. In ذَنْبَيْكَ العَظِيمَيْنِ, the type for both ذَنْبَيْ and العَظِيمَيْنِ is _____.

10. In ذُنُوبُكَ العَظِيمَةُ, the gender for both ذُنُوبُ and العَظِيمَةُ is _____.

B | Fill in the blanks using the word bank.

> After   Adjective   Sifah   Fragment   Singular   Properties
> Proper   Feminine   Mawsoof   Before   Described

1. Mawsoof Sifah is a kind of _____.

2. The Mawsoof is the word being _____ and the Sifah is the _____.

3. In English, the Sifah comes _____ the Mawsoof. But in Arabic, the Sifah comes _____ the Mawsoof.

4. The Mawsoof and Sifah have the same four _____.

5. In the fragment الْكِتَابَ الْقَيِّمَ, الْكِتَابَ is the _____ and الْقَيِّمَ is the _____. The four properties of both words are Nasb, _____, masculine, and _____.

6. Non-human plurals are always considered singular _____.

C | Translate the following fragments into Arabic using the word bank.

House	بَيْتٌ	Book	كِتَابٌ	Room	غُرْفَةٌ
Houses	بُيُوتٌ	Books	كُتُبٌ	Rooms	غُرَفٌ
New	جَدِيدٌ	Wide	وَاسِعٌ	Big	كَبِيرٌ

1. Your new book

2. Your two new books

3. Your new books

4. Their big house

5. Their two big houses

6. Their big houses

7. Her wide room

8. Her two wide rooms

9. Her wide rooms

10. In a new city

Date: _____

11. In two new cities

_____

12. In new cities

_____

13. In the new city

_____

14. In the two new cities

_____

15. In the new cities

_____

16. With a big book

_____

17. With two big books

_____

18. With big books

_____

19. With the big book

_____

20. With the two big books

_____

21. With the big books

_____

22. To the new house

_____

23. To the two new houses

_____

24. To the new houses

_____

Lesson 5

Accompanying Video
Unit 1: 1.12.1

Learning Goals • Practice identifying and translating all four fragments learned so far

A
Watch the accompanying video. Based on what you hear and see in the video, write/circle the correct answer.

1. In لَـٰكِنَّ عِبَادَاللَّهِ الْمُخْلَصِينَ, the اِسْمُ لَـٰكِنَّ is _____.

2. A Mudhaaf and a Mudhaaf Ilayh must always be right next to each other as do a Harf of Jarr and its victim. However a _____ doesn't necessarily have to be right next to its victim nor does a Mawsoof have to be right next to its Sifah.

3. الرَّحْمَـٰنِ and الرَّحِيمِ are both _____ of رَبِّ.

4. بِسْمِ is a _____ fragment.
   A. Mudhaaf and Mudhaaf Ilayh   B. Harf Jarr   C. Harf Nasb   D. Mawsoof Sifah

5. In the Mudhaaf/Mudhaaf Ilayh fragment ذِي قُوَّةٍ, the word ذِي is _____ in type.

6. عِنْدَ is a _____.

7. آيَاتُ الْكِتَابِ is a _____ fragment.
   A. Mudhaaf and Mudhaaf Ilayh   B. Harf Jarr   C. Harf Nasb   D. Mawsoof Sifah

8. الْعَرْشِ الْعَظِيمِ is a _____ fragment.
   A. Mudhaaf and Mudhaaf Ilayh   B. Harf Jarr   C. Harf Nasb   D. Mawsoof Sifah

Bayyinah Institute • Chapter 5

B Identify the different fragments in each of the phrases below. Write 'none' next to the fragments that are not present.

$$\text{لَـٰكِنَّ عِبَادَ اللَّهِ الْمُخْلَصِينَ}$$

Harf Jarr: _____   Idhaafah: _____

Harf Nasb: _____   Mawsoof Sifah: _____

$$\text{بِسْمِ اللَّهِ الرَّحْمَـٰنِ الرَّحِيمِ}$$

Harf Jarr: _____بِسْمِ_____   Idhaafah: _____

Harf Nasb: _____   Mawsoof Sifah: _____

$$\text{إِنَّهُ لَقَوْلُ رَسُولٍ كَرِيمٍ}$$

Harf Jarr: _____   Idhaafah: _____

Harf Nasb: _____   Mawsoof Sifah: _____

138   Chapter 5 • Bayyinah Institute

Date: _____

مِن رَّبِّ العَالَمِينَ

Harf Jarr: _____   Idhaafah: _____

Harf Nasb: _____   Mawsoof Sifah: _____

آيَاتُ الكِتَابِ المُبِينِ

Harf Jarr: _____   Idhaafah: _____

Harf Nasb: _____   Mawsoof Sifah: _____

لِلَّهِ غَيْبُ السَّمَاوَاتِ وَالأَرْضِ

Harf Jarr: _____   Idhaafah: _____

Harf Nasb: _____   Mawsoof Sifah: _____

كَأَنَّهُمْ أَعْجَازُ نَخْلٍ مُّنقَعِرٍ

Harf Jarr: _____   Idhaafah: _____

Harf Nasb: _____   Mawsoof Sifah: _____

C — Translate the following fragments into English using the word bank.

House بَيْتٌ/بُيُوتٌ	Worker عَامِلٌ	New جَدِيدٌ
City مَدِينَةٌ/مُدُنٌ	Visitor زَائِرٌ	Good صَالِحٌ
Book كِتَابٌ/كُتُبٌ	Teacher مُعَلِّمٌ	Big كَبِيرٌ

1. إِلَى مُدُنِهِمْ الكَبِيرَة

2. مَعَ كِتَابِ المُعَلِّمَةِ الجَدِيدَيْنِ

3. مَعَ كِتَابِ المُعَلِّمَةِ الجَدِيدَةِ

4. فِي بُيُوتِ العَامِلِينَ الصَّالِحِينَ

5. فِي بُيُوتِ العَامِلِينَ الجَدِيدَةِ

6. إِنَّ مَدِينَتِي الكَبِيرَة

7. لَكِنَّ مَدِينَةَ الزَّائِرَيْنِ الجَدِيدَيْنِ

8. عَنْ كِتَابِ مُعَلِّمَتِكَ الصَّالِحَةِ

9. عَنْ كِتَابِ مُعَلِّمَتِكَ الجَدِيدِ

10. عَنْ كُتُبِ مُعَلِّمَتَيْكَ الجَدِيدَةِ

D | Translate the following fragments into Arabic using the word bank.

1. Indeed, her teachers

2. Between the two new workers

3. As though her new teacher

4. In my big city

5. From the big houses

6. However, his big house

7. With the two new visitors

8. With his big books

9. For the two new teachers

10. With the big books

11. For his good workers

12. To your two new houses

Qur'anic Application

Circle all of the Mawsoof Sifah fragments below.

تَبَارَكَ الَّذِي بِيَدِهِ الْمُلْكُ وَهُوَ عَلَىٰ كُلِّ شَيْءٍ قَدِيرٌ ۝١ الَّذِي خَلَقَ الْمَوْتَ وَالْحَيَاةَ لِيَبْلُوَكُمْ أَيُّكُمْ أَحْسَنُ عَمَلًا ۚ وَهُوَ الْعَزِيزُ الْغَفُورُ ۝٢ الَّذِي خَلَقَ سَبْعَ سَمَاوَاتٍ طِبَاقًا ۖ مَّا تَرَىٰ فِي خَلْقِ الرَّحْمَٰنِ مِن تَفَاوُتٍ ۖ فَارْجِعِ الْبَصَرَ هَلْ تَرَىٰ مِن فُطُورٍ ۝٣ ثُمَّ ارْجِعِ الْبَصَرَ كَرَّتَيْنِ يَنقَلِبْ إِلَيْكَ الْبَصَرُ خَاسِئًا وَهُوَ حَسِيرٌ ۝٤ وَلَقَدْ زَيَّنَّا السَّمَاءَ الدُّنْيَا بِمَصَابِيحَ وَجَعَلْنَاهَا رُجُومًا لِّلشَّيَاطِينِ ۖ وَأَعْتَدْنَا لَهُمْ عَذَابَ السَّعِيرِ ۝٥ وَلِلَّذِينَ كَفَرُوا بِرَبِّهِمْ عَذَابُ جَهَنَّمَ ۖ وَبِئْسَ الْمَصِيرُ ۝٦

CHAPTER 6
Pointers

Chapter 6

The Ism Ishara اِسْمُ الإِشَارَةِ وَ مُشَارٌ إِلَيْهِ fragment is used to point to an Ism, e.g. this boy. It is comprised of two parts:

1) **Ism Ishara:** The pointing word, e.g. this, that.

2) **Mushaar Ilayh:** An Ism being pointed at.

Example

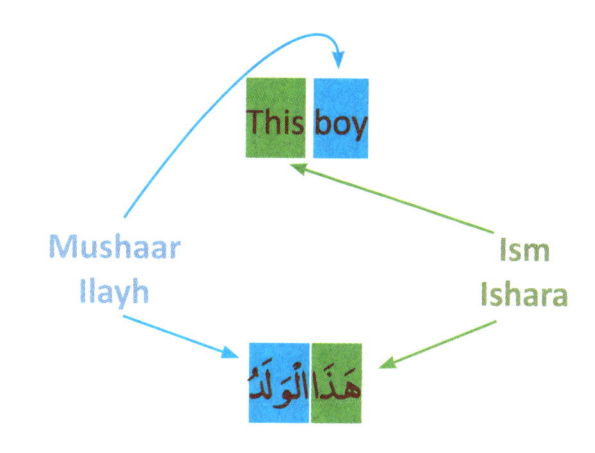

Mushaar Ilayh → This boy ← *Ism Ishara*

هَذَا الْوَلَدُ

The Ism Ishara

The following are the Isms used to point at something **near**:

PLURAL These	PAIR Both of these	SINGULAR This	STATUS	
هَـٰؤُلَاءِ	هَـٰذَانِ	هَـٰذَا	Raf' رفع	Masculine
	هَـٰذَيْنِ		Nasb نصب Jarr جرّ	
	هَاتَانِ	هَـٰذِهِ	Raf' رفع	Feminine
	هَاتَيْنِ		Nasb نصب Jarr جرّ	

The following are the Isms used to point at something **far**:

STATUS		SINGULAR This	PAIR Both of these	PLURAL These	
رفع	Raf'	ذٰلِكَ	ذَانِكَ	أُولَٰئِكَ	Masculine
نصب جرّ	Nasb Jarr		ذَيْنِكَ		
رفع	Raf'	تِلْكَ	تَانِكَ		Feminine
نصب جرّ	Nasb Jarr		تَيْنِكَ		

Recall the seven reasons for an Ism to be proper. Ism Ishara (pointing words) is one of those seven, thus Ism Ishara are always proper.

Rules for Ism Ishara Fragment

1) The Ism Ishara and the Mushaar Ilayh must match in all four properties.
2) The Mushaar Ilayh must have ال, e.g. الوَلَدُ.
3) Nothing can come between Ism Ishara and the Mushaar Ilayh.

Application

Are the following Ism Ishara fragments?

هَذَا الكِتَابُ

- ✓ All four properties match (Raf', Singular, Masculine, Proper)
- ✓ Mushaar Ilayh (الكِتَابُ) has ال
- ✓ Nothing between Ism Ishara and Mushaar Ilayh

Translation: This book

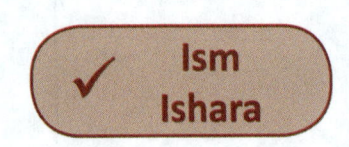

✓ **Ism Ishara**

مِنْ هَذَا الكِتَابِ

✓ Ism Ishara

- ✓ All four properties match (Jarr, Singular, Masculine, Proper)
- ✓ Mushaar Ilayh (الكِتَابِ) has ال
- ✓ Nothing between Ism Ishara and Mushaar Ilayh

Translation: From this book

هَذَا كِتَابٌ

✗ Ism Ishara

- ✗ All four properties do not match: هَذَا is proper, كِتَابٌ is common
- ✗ Mushaar Ilayh (كِتَابٌ) doesn't have ال

هَذَا مُحَمَّدٌ

✗ Ism Ishara

- ✓ All four properties match (Raf', Singular, Masculine, Proper)
- ✗ Mushaar Ilayh (مُحَمَّدٌ) doesn't have ال

Fragment or Sentence?

How do you translate the last two aforementioned examples?

هَذَا كِتَابٌ – This **is** a book.
هَذَا مُحَمَّدٌ – This **is** Muhammad.

Notice that the translations have the word "is", which is invisible in Arabic. Whenever we have this invisible "is", we have a sentence, not a fragment. We will learn more about the invisible "is" in the next module, insha Allah.

Rule for Determining Fragment or Sentence

For this chapter, understand this important rule:

If a Mushaar Ilayh doesn't have ال, it is not a fragment; it is a sentence.

Application

Are the following fragments or sentences?

هَذَا الكِتَابُ

- ✓ Mushaar Ilayh (الكِتَابُ) has ال, so it is a fragment.

Translation: This book

✓ Fragment

هَذَا كِتَابٌ

- ✗ Mushaar Ilayh (كِتَابٌ) doesn't have ال, so it is a sentence.

Translation: This is a book

✗ Fragment

Lesson 1

Accompanying Video
Unit 1: 1.13.1

Learning Goals • Memorize the pointers with their meaning • Know their four properties

A Watch the accompanying video. Based on what you hear and see in the video, write/circle the correct answer.

1. اِسْمُ الإِشَارَةِ and مُشَارٌ إِلَيْهِ are called _____ in English.

2. هَذَا means '_____'.

3. هَؤُلَاءِ means '_____'.

4. هَذِهِ means '_____' or those (when talking about non-human or broken plurals).

5. ذَلِكَ means '_____'.

6. أُولَآءِكَ means '_____'.

7. تِلْكَ means '_____' or those (when talking about non-human or broken plurals).

8. هَذَا, هَؤُلَاءِ, هَذِهِ, ذَلِكَ, أُولَآءِكَ, تِلْكَ all look the same whether they are in Raf', Nasb, or Jarr statuses, which means they are _____ words.

9. The type for all of these pointing words will always be _____.

Bayyinah Institute • Chapter 6

Date: _____

B | Write the pointers in the same order as you learned them in the video.

هَتَانِ هَؤُلَاءِ أُولَائِكَ هَذِهِ ذَلِكَ أُولَائِكَ

تِلْكَ هَذَا تَانِكَ هَذَانِ هَؤُلَاءِ ذَانِكَ

_____   _____   _____

_____   _____   _____

_____   _____   _____

_____   _____   _____

C | Match each word with its meaning.

A. This (f)   1. هَتَانِ

B. Both of those   2. هَذَا

C. These   3. أُولَآءِكَ

D. That   4. هَذِهِ

E. This   5. ذَانِكَ

F. Both of these (f)   6. ذَلِكَ

G. Those   7. هَذَانِ

H. That (f)   8. تَانِكَ

I. Both of these   9. تِلْكَ

J. Both of those (f)   10. هَؤُلَآءِ

D | Write the Raf', Nasb, and Jarr versions of each of the following pointers.

1. هَذَا

_____ (Raf') _____ (Nasb) _____ (Jarr)

2. هَذَانِ

_____ (Raf') _____ (Nasb) _____ (Jarr)

3. هَؤُلَاءِ

_____ (Raf') _____ (Nasb) _____ (Jarr)

4. هَتَيْنِ

_____ (Raf') _____ (Nasb) _____ (Jarr)

5. ذَلِكَ

_____ (Raf') _____ (Nasb) _____ (Jarr)

6. ذَيْنِكَ

_____ (Raf') _____ (Nasb) _____ (Jarr)

7. أُولَائِكَ

_____ (Raf') _____ (Nasb) _____ (Jarr)

8. تِلْكَ

_____ (Raf') _____ (Nasb) _____ (Jarr)

E | Write the four properties of each of the following pointers.

Date: _____

1. هَذَا

_____ (Type) _____ (Gender) _____ (Number) _____ (Status)

2. هَذَانِ

_____ (Type) _____ (Gender) _____ (Number) _____ (Status)

3. هَؤُلَاءِ

_____ (Type) _____ (Gender) _____ (Number) _____ (Status)

4. هَتَيْنِ

_____ (Type) _____ (Gender) _____ (Number) _____ (Status)

5. ذَٰلِكَ

_____ (Type) _____ (Gender) _____ (Number) _____ (Status)

6. ذَيْنِكَ

_____ (Type) _____ (Gender) _____ (Number) _____ (Status)

7. أُولَٰئِكَ

_____ (Type) _____ (Gender) _____ (Number) _____ (Status)

8. تِلْكَ

_____ (Type) _____ (Gender) _____ (Number) _____ (Status)

F | Circle the pointer in each question.

1. A. هَذَا
   B. الَّذِينَ
   C. فِرْعَوْنَ
   D. هُوَ

2. A. أَنْتَ
   B. الَّذِي
   C. مِلَّةَ
   D. هَتَيْنِ

3. A. اللَّتَانِ
   B. هُمْ
   C. هُمَا
   D. هَذِهِ

4. A. اللَّاتِي
   B. أَنْتُمْ
   C. هَذَانِ
   D. فِي

5. A. تَيْنِكَ
   B. الَّذِي
   C. أَنْتُنَّ
   D. إِلَى

6. A. عَنْ
   B. هَؤُلَاءِ
   C. اللَّتَانِ
   D. هُنَّ

7. A. أَنَا
   B. تِلْكَ
   C. اللَّذَانِ
   D. حَقٍّ

8. A. تَانِكَ
   B. هُمْ
   C. بَيْتٌ
   D. نَحْنُ

9. A. الَّتِي
   B. عَلَى
   C. هِيَ
   D. أُولَائِكَ

10. A. ذَلِكَ
    B. هُمَا
    C. الَّذِي
    D. هُنَّ

11. A. أَنْتِ
    B. ذَيْنِكَ
    C. بَيْنَ
    D. حَتَّى

12. A. أَنَّ
    B. تَ
    C. هَذَيْنِ
    D. أَنْتُمَا

G | Find all of the pointers in the ayahs below.

1. ذَٰلِكَ الْكِتَابُ لَا رَيْبَ ۛ فِيهِ ۛ هُدًى لِّلْمُتَّقِينَ ﴿٢﴾

2. أُولَٰئِكَ عَلَىٰ هُدًى مِّن رَّبِّهِمْ ۖ وَأُولَٰئِكَ هُمُ الْمُفْلِحُونَ ﴿٥﴾

3. وَتِلْكَ عَادٌ ۖ جَحَدُوا بِآيَاتِ رَبِّهِمْ وَعَصَوْا رُسُلَهُ وَاتَّبَعُوا أَمْرَ كُلِّ جَبَّارٍ عَنِيدٍ ﴿٥٩﴾

4. ثُمَّ عَفَوْنَا عَنكُم مِّن بَعْدِ ذَٰلِكَ لَعَلَّكُمْ تَشْكُرُونَ ﴿٥٢﴾

5. قَالَ الْمَلَأُ مِن قَوْمِ فِرْعَوْنَ إِنَّ هَٰذَا لَسَاحِرٌ عَلِيمٌ ﴿١٠٩﴾

6. فَمَا زَالَت تِّلْكَ دَعْوَاهُمْ حَتَّىٰ جَعَلْنَاهُمْ حَصِيدًا خَامِدِينَ ﴿١٥﴾

7. قَالُوا إِنْ هَٰذَانِ لَسَاحِرَانِ يُرِيدَانِ أَن يُخْرِجَاكُم مِّنْ أَرْضِكُم بِسِحْرِهِمَا... ﴿٦٣﴾

8. وَقَضَيْنَا إِلَيْهِ ذَٰلِكَ الْأَمْرَ أَنَّ دَابِرَ هَٰؤُلَاءِ مَقْطُوعٌ مُّصْبِحِينَ ﴿٦٦﴾

9. وَتِلْكَ الْجَنَّةُ الَّتِي أُورِثْتُمُوهَا بِمَا كُنتُمْ تَعْمَلُونَ ﴿٧٢﴾

10. أُولَٰئِكَ عَلَيْهِمْ صَلَوَاتٌ مِّن رَّبِّهِمْ وَرَحْمَةٌ ۖ وَأُولَٰئِكَ هُمُ الْمُهْتَدُونَ ﴿١٥٧﴾

Lesson 2

Accompanying Video
Unit 1: 1.13.2

Learning Goals • Know how to make a fragment or sentence with pointers

A Watch the accompanying video. Based on what you hear and see in the video, write/circle the correct answer.

1. 'This toy' is a _____ while 'This is a toy' is a complete sentence.

2. In _____ they don't have the word 'is' or 'are'.

3. If you have a pointer and right after that is a word with ال on it, it will be a _____ and there is no invisible 'is' or 'are'.

4. If you have a pointer and right after that is a word without any ال on it, it will be a _____ and there is an invisible 'is' or 'are'.

5. هَذَا القُرْآنُ is translated as '_____'.

6. هَذَا كِتَابٌ is translated as '_____'.

7. تِلْكَ الرُّسُلُ is translated as '_____'.

8. تِلْكَ آيَاتُ الكِتَابِ is translated as '_____'.

9. هَذِهِ الحَيَاةُ is translated as '_____'.

Bayyinah Institute • Chapter 6

B Fill in the blanks using the word bank.

> Proper   Sentences   Isms   Fragment   Singular
> Non-flexible   ال   ذَانِكَ   ذَيْنِكَ   Meaning

1. Pointers are _____; so they have four properties.

2. The singular and plural pointers are _____; so their Raf', Nasb, and Jarr versions are the same.

3. The Raf', Nasb, and Jarr version of ذَانِكَ are _____, _____ , and ذَيْنِكَ .

4. You can tell the number and gender of pointers by their _____. So the number and gender of هَذَا is _____ masculine.

5. Pointers are always _____.

6. Pointers can make fragments or _____.

7. If the word right after the pointer has a(n) _____, then it makes a fragment.

8. هَذَا المَسْجِدُ is a _____ and هَذَا مَسْجِدٌ is a sentence.

C. Write an 'F' next to the fragments and an 'S' next to the sentences in the following questions.

1. This cat
2. Those houses
3. This is a mansion
4. Those two cars
5. These hard lessons
6. This is my pet
7. Tall plants
8. New desk
9. Fast cars
10. This building
11. This ocean
12. Those two chairs
13. This big glass
14. That is my book
15. This Messenger
16. That house
17. Beautiful art
18. Creator of the universe
19. Comfortable couch
20. Healthy children
21. That moment
22. All of these students
23. This is her palace
24. Those people
25. That smart girl
26. This is a sign
27. These desks
28. Those are his pens
29. This country
30. These two friends

D | Identify if each of the following is a sentence or a fragment.

1. هَذِهِ أَنْعَامٌ — **Sentence**
2. هَذِهِ الشَّجَرَةُ — _____
3. هَذِهِ الدُّنْيَا — _____
4. تِلْكَ الدَّارُ — _____
5. هَذِهِ الْقَرْيَةُ — _____
6. ذَلِكَ خَيْرٌ — _____
7. هَذَا بَلَدٌ — _____
8. هَذَا الْقُرْآنُ — _____
9. هَذَا رَبِّي — _____
10. ذَلِكَ أَدْنَى — _____

11. ذَلِكَ الْكِتَابُ — _____
12. هَذِهِ الْحَيَاةُ — _____
13. هَذِهِ بِضَاعَتُنَا — _____
14. هَذَا لَسَاحِرٌ عَلِيمٌ — _____
15. هَؤُلَاءِ شُفَعَاؤُنَا — _____
16. تِلْكَ أُمَّةٌ — _____
17. هَذِهِ نَاقَةُ اللَّهِ — _____
18. هَذَا صِرَاطٌ — _____
19. هَذَانِ خَصْمَانِ — _____
20. هَذِهِ التَّمَاثِيلُ — _____

E | Translate the following fragments into English using the word bank.

House	بَيْتٌ/بُيُوتٌ	Worker	عَامِلٌ	New	جَدِيدٌ
City	مَدِينَةٌ/مُدُنٌ	Visitor	زَائِرٌ	Good	صَالِحٌ
Book	كِتَابٌ/كُتُبٌ	Teacher	مُعَلِّمٌ	Big	كَبِيرٌ

1. ذَلِكَ المُعَلِّمُ

6. إِنَّ هَذَا المُعَلِّمَ

2. أُولَائِكَ المُعَلِّمُونَ

7. لَكِنَّ هَذِهِ البُيُوتِ الجَدِيدَةِ

3. تِلْكَ العَامِلَةُ

8. عَنْ هَذَيْنِ الأُسْتَاذَيْنِ

4. تَانِكَ العَامِلَتَانِ

9. إِلَى هَؤُلَاءِ الزَّائِرِينَ

5. هَذِهِ المَدِينَةُ

10. مَعَ تِلْكَ الكُتُبِ الجَدِيدَةِ

BUILDING VOCABULARY

Bayyinah Institute • Chapter 6

161

F | Translate the following fragments into Arabic using the word bank.

1. This book

2. That new book

3. These two books

4. Those two new books

5. These books

6. Those new books

7. That city

8. This big city

9. Those two cities

10. These two big cities

11. Those cities

12. These big cities

Lesson 3

Accompanying Video
Unit 1: 1.13.3

Learning Goals • Practice identifying when pointers make a fragment or sentence

A | Watch the accompanying video. Based on what you hear and see in the video, write/circle the correct answer.

1. ذَلِكَ الْكِتَابُ is translated as '_____'.

2. هَذِهِ الشَّجَرَةُ is translated as '_____'.

3. ذَلِكَ أَدْنَى is translated as '_____'.

4. الدَّارُ is feminine because '_____'.

5. أُولَٰٓئِكَ أَصْحَابُ النَّارِ is translated as '_____'.

6. هَذَا الَّذِي is translated as '_____'.

7. تِلْكَ أُمَّةٌ is translated as '_____'.

8. هَٰؤُلَاءِ شُفَعَاؤُنَا is translated as '_____ intercessors'.

9. هَذَا رَبِّي is translated as '_____'.

10. هَذَانِ خَصْمَانِ is translated as '_____'.

B | Fill in the blanks using the word bank.

> Shouldn't   Sentences   Fragments   Same   Should   Properties
> Non-flexible   ذَلِكَ مَسْجِدٌ   ذَلِكَ الْمَسْجِدُ   هَذَيْنِ   هَذَانِ

1. The singular and plural pointers are _____, so their Raf', Nasb, and Jarr versions are the _____.

2. The Raf', Nasb, and Jarr versions of the pointer هَذَانِ are _____, هَذَيْنِ, and _____.

3. Pointers can make _____ or _____.

4. To make a fragment, the word immediately after the pointer _____ have ال. To make a sentence, the word after the pointer _____ have ال.

5. _____ is a fragment and _____ is a sentence.

6. When making a fragment, the four _____ of the pointer and 'the pointed at' (the word after it) must match.

Chapter 6 • Bayyinah Institute

C | Write the four properties of each of the following Isms.

1. هَذَا القَلَمُ

Sentence or fragment? _____

هَذَا
_____ _____ _____ _____
(Status)   (Number)   (Gender)   (Type)

القَلَمُ
_____ _____ _____ _____
(Status)   (Number)   (Gender)   (Type)

2. تِلْكَ شَجَرَةٌ

Sentence or fragment? _____

تِلْكَ
_____ _____ _____ _____
(Status)   (Number)   (Gender)   (Type)

شَجَرَةٌ
_____ _____ _____ _____
(Status)   (Number)   (Gender)   (Type)

3. هَذِهِ البُيُوتُ

Sentence or fragment? _____

هَذِهِ
_____ _____ _____ _____
(Status)   (Number)   (Gender)   (Type)

البُيُوتُ
_____ _____ _____ _____
(Status)   (Number)   (Gender)   (Type)

Bayyinah Institute • Chapter 6

Date: _____

4. أُولَٰئِكَ الْمُعَلِّمُونَ

Sentence or fragment? _____

أُولَٰئِكَ
_____ _____ _____ _____
(Status)   (Number)   (Gender)   (Type)

الْمُعَلِّمُونَ
_____ _____ _____ _____
(Status)   (Number)   (Gender)   (Type)

5. هَٰذَيْنِ خَصْمَيْنِ

Sentence or fragment? _____

هَٰذَيْنِ
_____ _____ _____ _____
(Status)   (Number)   (Gender)   (Type)

خَصْمَيْنِ
_____ _____ _____ _____
(Status)   (Number)   (Gender)   (Type)

6. هَٰذِهِ نَارٌ

Sentence or fragment? _____

هَٰذِهِ
_____ _____ _____ _____
(Status)   (Number)   (Gender)   (Type)

نَارٌ
_____ _____ _____ _____
(Status)   (Number)   (Gender)   (Type)

Date: _____

D | **Identify if each of the following pointers makes a fragment or a sentence, then translate each to complete the translation given.**
Hint: If it is a sentence, make sure you add an 'is'/'are' after the pointer.

1. ____That is____ a book   S   F   ١. ذَٰلِكَ كِتَابٌ

2. _____ worldly life   S   F   ٢. هَـٰذِهِ الحَيَاةَ الدُّنْيَا

3. _____ the companions of Paradise   S   F   ٣. أُولَـٰٓئِكَ أَصْحَابُ الجَنَّةِ

4. _____ my Lord   S   F   ٤. هَـٰذَا رَبِّي

5. _____ the limits set by Allah   S   F   ٥. تِلْكَ حُدُودُ اللَّهِ

6. _____ our intercessors   S   F   ٦. هَـٰؤُلَآءِ شُفَعَاؤُنَا

7. _____ a straight path   S   F   ٧. هَـٰذَا صِرَاطٌ مُّسْتَقِيمٌ

8. _____ arguers/opponents   S   F   ٨. هَـٰذَانِ خَصْمَانِ

9. _____ the she-camel of Allah   S   F   ٩. هَـٰذِهِ نَاقَةُ اللَّهِ

10. _____ cattle   S   F   ١٠. هَـٰذِهِ أَنْعَامٌ

Bayyinah Institute • Chapter 6

E | **Translate the following fragments into Arabic using the word bank.**

House	بَيْتٌ/بُيُوتٌ	Worker	عَامِلٌ	New	جَدِيدٌ
City	مَدِينَةٌ/مُدُنٌ	Visitor	زَائِرٌ	Good	صَالِحٌ
Book	كِتَابٌ/كُتُبٌ	Teacher	مُعَلِّمٌ	Big	كَبِيرٌ

1. That big house

2. That is a big house.

3. This new worker

4. This is a new worker.

5. These two good female teachers

6. These are two good female teachers.

7. These books

8. These are his books.

9. To those two houses

10. To those two new houses

Qur'anic Application

Circle the pointers in the following ayahs.

تَبَارَكَ الَّذِي بِيَدِهِ الْمُلْكُ وَهُوَ عَلَىٰ كُلِّ شَيْءٍ قَدِيرٌ ﴿١﴾ الَّذِي خَلَقَ الْمَوْتَ وَالْحَيَاةَ لِيَبْلُوَكُمْ أَيُّكُمْ أَحْسَنُ عَمَلًا ۚ وَهُوَ الْعَزِيزُ الْغَفُورُ ﴿٢﴾ الَّذِي خَلَقَ سَبْعَ سَمَاوَاتٍ طِبَاقًا ۖ مَّا تَرَىٰ فِي خَلْقِ الرَّحْمَٰنِ مِن تَفَاوُتٍ ۖ فَارْجِعِ الْبَصَرَ هَلْ تَرَىٰ مِن فُطُورٍ ﴿٣﴾ ثُمَّ ارْجِعِ الْبَصَرَ كَرَّتَيْنِ يَنقَلِبْ إِلَيْكَ الْبَصَرُ خَاسِئًا وَهُوَ حَسِيرٌ ﴿٤﴾ وَلَقَدْ زَيَّنَّا السَّمَاءَ الدُّنْيَا بِمَصَابِيحَ وَجَعَلْنَاهَا رُجُومًا لِّلشَّيَاطِينِ ۖ وَأَعْتَدْنَا لَهُمْ عَذَابَ السَّعِيرِ ﴿٥﴾ وَلِلَّذِينَ كَفَرُوا بِرَبِّهِمْ عَذَابُ جَهَنَّمَ ۖ وَبِئْسَ الْمَصِيرُ ﴿٦﴾

Frag-

Harf + Ism

Harf Jarr

Construction
Harf Jarr + Ism

Rules
- Harf Jarr makes the Ism after it in Jarr status
- Harf of Jarr and its Ism must be next to each other

Harf Jarrs:
بـ تـ كـ لـ و مِنْ فِيْ عَنْ عَلَى حَتَّى إِلَى

Harf Nasb

Construction
Harf Nasb + Ism

Rules
- Harf Nasb makes the Ism in Nasb status
- Harf of Nasb and its Ism do not have to be next to each other

Harf Nasbs:
إِنَّ أَنَّ كَأَنَّ لَيْتَ لَكِنَّ لَعَلَّ بِأَنَّ لِأَنَّ

ments

Ism + Ism

Idhaafah

Construction
Mudhaaf + Mudhaaf Ilayh

Rules
- Mudhaaf = word before 'of':
  1. Light,
  2. No ال
- Mudhaaf Ilayh = word after 'of':
  1. Always in Jarr status
- Mudhaaf and Mudhaaf Ilayh must be next to each other

Mawsoof Sifah

Construction
Mawsoof + Sifah

Rules
- Mawsoof = noun
- Sifah = adjective
- Mawsoof comes first
- All four properties of Sifah must match all four properties of Mawsoof
- You can have more than one Sifah

Pointers

Construction
Ism Ishaarah + Mushaar Ilayh

Rules
- Ism Ishaarah = pointing word
- Mushaar Ilayh = word being pointed at
- Ism Ishaarah must be followed by ال. If there is no ال it makes a sentence
- All four properties of Ism Ishaarah match all four properties of Mushaar Ilayh
- Ism Ishaarah and Mushaar Ilayh must be next to each other

MODULE 3
Sentences

CHAPTER 1

The Invisible 'Is'
Making sentences using Isms and fragments. Five ways to find the invisible 'is' that makes a sentence.

CHAPTER 2

Surah Kahf
Apply learned grammar concepts of Isms and Harfs and the fragments they make in the first 10 ayahs of the Surah.

CHAPTER 1
The Invisible 'Is'

Chapter 1

Recall from the last chapter, we translated هَذَا كِتَابٌ as "This **is** a book." We discussed that the translation has the word "is", which is invisible in Arabic. Whenever we have this invisible "is", we have an Arabic sentence!

There are two types of sentences in Arabic:

1) Jumlah Ismiyyah الجُمْلَةُ الاِسْمِيَّةُ – a sentence that begins with an Ism in Raf' status; it has the invisible "is".

2) Jumlah Fi'liyyah الجُمْلَةُ الفِعْلِيَّةُ – anytime you have a Fi'l, you have a Jumlah Fi'liyyah.

هَذَا كِتَابٌ as "This **is** a book" is a Jumlah Ismiyyah. We will discuss Jumlah Ismiyyah in this chapter and explore Jumlah Fi'liyyah in the next, insha Allah. In case you are wondering, there is no Jumlah Harfiyyah!

Finding the Invisible "is" To Understand Jumlah Ismiyyah

In Arabic, there is no way to say "is" or any of its variants (am, are). **In other words, the "is" is invisible in a Jumlah Ismiyyah.** To understand the Jumlah Ismiyyah, we have to find the invisible "is".

There is one golden rule we can use to find the invisible "is" in a Jumlah Ismiyyah: 'the break in the chain' rule.

The Break in the Chain

Recall that fragments are two words that are chained together by a grammar rule. Once we find two words that are not connected to each other by one of the five fragments, there is a break in the chain. That is where the invisible "is" goes.

Examples

هَذَا كِتَابٌ

- هَذَا and كِتَابٌ are not chained together by any fragment so the invisible "is" will be between them.
- Translation: هَذَا is كِتَابٌ i.e. This is a book.

الْحَمْدُ لِلَّهِ

- الْحَمْدُ and لِلَّهِ are not chained together by any fragment, even though بِهِ is a Jaar Majroor fragment, so the invisible "is" will be between them.
- Translation: الْحَمْدُ is لِلَّهِ i.e. Praise is for Allah.

Common Breaks in the Chain

Four beaks in the chain occur frequently:

1. Proper Ism followed by common Ism

اَللَّهُ غَفُورٌ

اَللَّهُ is غَفُورٌ i.e. Allah is forgiving.

2. Immediately after an independent pronoun

أَنَا خَيْرٌ مِنْهُ

أَنَا am خَيْرٌ مِنْهُ i.e. I am better than him

Note that we are only looking for one break in the chain as a sentence has one "is" in it.

3. Right after a Harf Nasb and its Ism

إِنَّ رَحْمَةَ اللَّهِ قَرِيبٌ

إِنَّ رَحْمَةَ اللَّهِ is قَرِيبٌ i.e. Certainly Allah's mercy is close.

Note that إِنَّ and رَحْمَةَ are chained by Harf Nasb, then رَحْمَةَ and اللَّهِ are chained by Idhaafah.

4. An Ism Ishara with no ال after it

هَذَا مُحَمَّدٌ

هَذَا is مُحَمَّدٌ i.e. This is Muhammad.

Lesson 1

Accompanying Video
Unit 1: 1.14.1

Learning Goals • Know how to find the invisible 'is'/'are'

A | Watch the accompanying video. Based on what you hear and see in the video, write/circle the correct answer.

1. The first way to find the invisible 'is' in Arabic is to look for words that are proper followed by _____ words.

2. Whenever you see هُوَ, it actually doesn't mean 'he', it means '_____'.

3. Anytime you see a _____ and its Ism, there will automatically be an 'is' after them.

4. The fourth way to find the invisible 'is' is if you see an Ism Ishaarah followed by any word that doesn't have _____.

5. In الحَمْدُ لِلَّهِ, the invisible 'is' comes after the word _____.

6. بِسْمِ اللَّهِ الرَّحْمَنِ الرَّحِيمِ is a _____ because there is no break in the chain.

7. The easiest way to find the invisible 'is' in the sentence هُوَ اللَّهُ is through _____.

    A. Proper followed by common   B. Original pronoun   C. Harf of Nasb and its Ism

8. In إِنَّ رَحْمَةَ اللَّهِ قَرِيبٌ, the invisible 'is' comes after the word _____.

Bayyinah Institute • Chapter 1

B | Fill in the blanks using the word bank.

> Sentences   Common   Idhaafah   Pointers   After
> Independent   Chained   Nasb   ال   Fragment

1. You learned five fragments: _____, Harf of Jarr, Harf of _____, Mawsoof Sifah, and _____.

2. _____ have an 'is' in them.

3. A proper Ism followed by a(n) _____ Ism is a way to find the invisible 'is.'

4. Every time you see a(n) _____ pronoun, it will be followed by an invisible 'is.'

5. There is an 'is' _____ a Harf Nasb and its victim.

6. If the word after a pointer doesn't have _____, then there is an 'is' between the pointer and the word after it.

7. Different parts of a fragment are _____ together. A break in the chain happens when two words don't make a _____, and that is where you put the invisible 'is.'

C | Match each fragment with its label. They have been divided up so 1-5 match with A-E, 6-10 match with F-J, and 11-15 match with K-O.

A. Harf Jarr   1. عَذَابٌ عَظِيمٌ

B. Harf Nasb   2. تَحْتَ الشَّجَرَةِ

C. Mawsoof Sifah   3. أَنَّهُ

D. Pointer   4. إِلَى السَّمَاءِ

E. Idhaafah   5. هَذَا الْبَيْتِ

F. Pointer   6. إِنَّ السَّاعَةَ

G. Harf Nasb   7. بُيُوتٌ كَبِيرَةٌ

H. Idhaafah   8. بِالْهُدَى

I. Harf Jarr   9. تِلْكَ الرُّسُلُ

J. Mawsoof Sifah   10. أَنْفُسَهُم

K. Harf Jarr   11. مَسْجِداً كَبِيراً

L. Mawsoof Sifah   12. هَذَانِ الْقَلَمَانِ

M. Pointer   13. بَيْنَ الْمَرْءِ

N. Idhaafah   14. لَعَلَّهُم

O. Harf Nasb   15. لِلْمُعَلِّمِينَ

D Identify if the two words make a fragment in each of the following questions. If they do, label what kind of fragment it is. If not, leave it blank.

1. إِنَّ اللَّهَ _____ 11. سَاحِرٌ عَلِيمٌ _____

2. إِلَيْهِمْ _____ 12. هُنَّ مُسْلِمَاتٌ _____

3. هَذِهِ الدُّنْيَا _____ 13. وَرَآئِهِمْ _____

4. لَعَلَّهُمْ _____ 14. كَالْعِهْنِ _____

5. بَيْنَ أَحَدٍ _____ 15. هُوَ قَرِيبٌ _____

6. ذَلِكَ خَيْرٌ _____ 16. تِلْكَ الْمُدُنُ _____

7. اللَّهُ قَادِرٌ _____ 17. صَيْحَةً وَاحِدَةً _____

8. هَذَا الْقُرْآنُ _____ 18. هُمْ فِي _____

9. رَسُولٍ كَرِيمٍ _____ 19. هَذَانِ خَصْمَانِ _____

10. يَوْمَ الْحَجِّ _____ 20. اللَّهُ أَكْبَرُ _____

E | Identify the different fragments in each of the following questions (not all questions will have two fragments). Mark where the invisible 'is'/'are' goes and translate using the definitions given.

هَذَا صِرَاطٌ مُّسْتَقِيمٌ

Fragment #1: _____ Fragment #2: _____

Translation: _____ Path: صِرَاطٌ Straight: مُسْتَقِيمٌ

ذَٰلِكَ مِنْ آيَاتِ اللَّهِ

Fragment #1: _____ Fragment #2: _____

Translation: _____ Signs: آيَاتِ

اَلْحَقُّ مِنْ رَّبِّكُمْ

Fragment #1: _____ Fragment #2: _____

Translation: _____ The truth: اَلْحَقُّ

BUILDING VOCABULARY

Date: _____

إِنِّي عَلَىٰ بَيِّنَةٍ

Fragment #1: _____ Fragment #2: _____

Translation: _____ Clear proof: بَيِّنَةٍ

تِلْكَ آيَاتُ الْكِتَابِ الْمُبِينِ

Fragment #1: _____ Fragment #2: _____

Translation: _____ Clear: الْمُبِينِ

لَكُمْ دِينُكُمْ

Fragment #1: _____ Fragment #2: _____

Translation: _____ Religion: دِينُ

F | Find the invisible 'is'/'are' in each of the following questions.

1. هَذَا صِرَاطٌ مُسْتَقِيمٌ
2. إِنَّهُمْ فِتْيَةٌ
3. رَبُّنَا رَبُّ السَّمَاوَاتِ
4. أُولَائِكَ أَصْحَابُ الْجَنَّةِ
5. فِي الْأَرْضِ قِطَعٌ مُتَجَاوِرَاتٌ
6. مِنْ طَلْعِهَا قِنْوَانٌ دَانِيَةٌ
7. إِنَّ بَطْشَ رَبِّكَ لَشَدِيدٌ
8. تِلْكَ حُدُودُ اللَّهِ
9. اَلظَّالِمُونَ فِي ضَلَالٍ مُبِينٍ
10. اَلْأَنْفَالُ لِلَّهِ
11. هَؤُلَاءِ شُفَعَاؤُنَا
12. كَأَنَّكَ حَفِيٌّ
13. هَذَانِ خَصْمَانِ
14. إِنَّ اللَّهَ قَادِرٌ
15. لَكِنِّي رَسُولٌ
16. أَنْتُمْ قَوْمٌ مُسْرِفُونَ
17. هَذِهِ نَاقَةُ اللَّهِ
18. كَأَنَّ فِي أُذُنَيْهِ وَقْراً
19. النُّجُومُ مُسَخَّرَاتٌ
20. بَعْضُهُمْ أَوْلِيَاءُ بَعْضٍ
21. هَذِهِ أَنْعَامٌ
22. الْحَقُّ مِنْ رَبِّكُمْ
23. أَنَا أَكْثَرُ مِنْكَ مَالًا
24. هُوَ الْغَفُورُ الْوَدُودُ
25. ذَلِكَ مِنْ آيَاتِ اللَّهِ
26. إِنَّ هَذِهِ تَذْكِرَةٌ
27. أَنَا رَبُّكَ
28. إِلَهُكُمْ إِلَهٌ وَاحِدٌ
29. مِنْ وَرَائِهِمْ مُحِيطٌ
30. اَلْحَمْدُ لِلَّهِ

Lesson 2

Accompanying Video
Unit 1: 1.14.2

Learning Goals • Practice finding the invisible 'is' and translating sentences

A Watch the accompanying video. Based on what you hear and see in the video, write/circle the correct answer.

1. The easiest way to find the invisible 'is' in the sentence إِنَّهُمْ فِتْيَةٌ is through _____.

   A. Proper followed by common   B. Original pronoun   C. Harf Nasb and its victim
   D. Ism Ishaarah followed by no ال   E. Break in the chain

2. Sometimes in Arabic, what looks like a Mawsoof Sifah can instead be a _____ with an 'is' in between, you just get used to that with experience.

3. The easiest way to find the invisible 'is' in the sentence تِلْكَ آيَاتُ الْكِتَابِ is through _____.

4. The easiest way to find the invisible 'is' in the sentence أَنْتُمْ قَوْمٌ مُسْرِفُونَ is through _____.

5. The easiest way to find the invisible 'is' in the sentence اللَّهُ مُحِيطٌ بِالْكَافِرِينَ is through _____.

6. أَنَّ الْقُوَّةَ لِلَّهِ is translated as '_____'.

7. أَنَّ فِيكُمْ رَسُولَ اللَّهِ is translated as '_____'.

Bayyinah Institute • Chapter 1   185

Date: _____

B | **Write out the five fragments and the five ways to find the invisible 'is' learned in the last lesson, then give an example of each.**

List the five fragments: Example:

1. _____ 1. _____

2. _____ 2. _____

3. _____ 3. _____

4. _____ 4. _____

5. _____ 5. _____

List the five ways to find the invisible 'is': Example:

1. _____ 1. _____

2. _____ 2. _____

3. _____ 3. _____

4. _____ 4. _____

5. _____ 5. _____

C

Determine if the following are sentences or fragments. If it is a sentence, find the invisible 'is' and write 'sentence'. If it is one or more fragments, label each fragment.

Hint: Some sentences have fragments in them, don't label those fragments.

1. هَذِهِ|أَنْعَامٌ — Sentence
2. هَذِهِ الشَّجَرَةُ — Pointer
3. تِلْكَ أُمَّةٌ
4. اَلْحَمْدُ لِلَّهِ
5. هَذِهِ الدُّنْيَا
6. لَهُ كُلُّ شَيْءٍ
7. إِنَّهُمْ فِتْيَةٌ
8. ذَلِكَ خَيْرٌ
9. وَعْدَ اللَّهِ
10. هَذَا رَبِّي

11. عَلَى أَهْلِ بَيْتٍ
12. إِنَّكَ عَلَى الْحَقِّ
13. هَذِهِ بِضَاعَتُنَا
14. مِنَ الْمُفْسِدِينَ
15. هَؤُلَاءِ شُفَعَاؤُنَا
16. وَعْدَ اللَّهِ حَقٌّ
17. هُمْ مُسْلِمُونَ
18. هَذَانِ خَصْمَانِ
19. اَلْحَقِّ الْمُبِينِ
20. وَلَكِنَّ أَكْثَرَهُمْ

D | Translate the following fragments/sentences into English using the word bank.

House	بَيْتٌ/بُيُوتٌ	Worker	عَامِلٌ	New	جَدِيدٌ
City	مَدِينَةٌ/مُدُنٌ	Visitor	زَائِرٌ	Good	صَالِحٌ
Book	كِتَابٌ/كُتُبٌ	Teacher	مُعَلِّمٌ	Big	كَبِيرٌ

1. هَذِهِ الْمَدِينَةُ كَبِيرَةٌ

2. هَذِهِ مَدِينَةٌ كَبِيرَةٌ

3. هَذِهِ مَدِينَتُهَا الْكَبِيرَةُ

4. تَانِكَ عَامِلَتَانِ صَالِحَتَانِ

5. تَانِكَ الْعَامِلَتَانِ الصَّالِحَتَانِ

6. إِلَى تَيْنِكَ الْعَامِلَتَيْنِ الصَّالِحَتَيْنِ

7. هُمَا عَامِلَتَانِ صَالِحَتَانِ

8. هُمْ مُعَلِّمُونَ صَالِحُونَ

9. هَؤُلَاءِ الْمُعَلِّمُونَ صَالِحُونَ

10. هَؤُلَاءِ مُعَلِّمُونَ صَالِحُونَ

E | Translate the following fragments/sentences into Arabic using the word bank.

1. She is a teacher

2. She is a new teacher

3. This teacher (f) is new

4. This is a new teacher (f)

5. Those new books

6. Those books are new

7. Those are new books

8. Those are his new books

9. These two big houses

10. These are two big houses

11. These two houses are big

12. These are his two big houses

BUILDING VOCABULARY

F | Identify the different fragments in each of the phrases below (not all questions will have two or three fragments). Mark where the invisible 'is' goes and translate using the definitions given.

Date: _____

إِنَّ اللَّهَ قَادِرٌ

Fragment #1: _____ Fragment #2: _____

Translation: _____ Capable: قَادِرٌ

أَنَّ وَعْدَ اللَّهِ حَقٌّ

Fragment #1: _____ Fragment #2: _____

Translation: _____ True: حَقٌّ Promise: وَعْدَ

إِنَّكَ عَلَى الْحَقِّ الْمُبِينِ

Fragment #1: _____ Fragment #2: _____

Fragment #3: _____

Translation: _____ Clear: الْمُبِين The truth: الْحَقِّ

Date: _____

إِنَّ هَـٰذِهِ تَذْكِرَةٌ

Fragment #1: _____ Fragment #2: _____

Translation: _____   A reminder: تَذْكِرَةٌ

إِنَّ لِلْمُتَّقِينَ مَفَازاً

Fragment #1: _____ Fragment #2: _____

Translation: _____   Success: مَفَازاً Good people: مُتَّقِينَ

أَنَّ فِيكُمْ رَسُولَ اللهِ

Fragment #1: _____ Fragment #2: _____

Fragment #3: _____

Translation: _____   Messenger: رَسُولَ   Among: فِي

BUILDING VOCABULARY

Important Concepts

Write the five ways to find the invisible 'is' in Arabic:

1. _____

2. _____

3. _____

4. _____

5. _____

Qur'anic Application

Find the invisible 'is' in each of the highlighted parts below.

تَبَارَكَ الَّذِي بِيَدِهِ الْمُلْكُ <mark>وَهُوَ عَلَىٰ كُلِّ شَيْءٍ قَدِيرٌ</mark> ﴿١﴾ الَّذِي خَلَقَ الْمَوْتَ وَالْحَيَاةَ لِيَبْلُوَكُمْ <mark>أَيُّكُمْ أَحْسَنُ عَمَلًا ۚ وَهُوَ الْعَزِيزُ الْغَفُورُ</mark> ﴿٢﴾ الَّذِي خَلَقَ سَبْعَ سَمَاوَاتٍ طِبَاقًا ۖ مَّا تَرَىٰ فِي خَلْقِ الرَّحْمَٰنِ مِن تَفَاوُتٍ ۖ فَارْجِعِ الْبَصَرَ هَلْ تَرَىٰ مِن فُطُورٍ ﴿٣﴾ ثُمَّ ارْجِعِ الْبَصَرَ كَرَّتَيْنِ يَنقَلِبْ إِلَيْكَ الْبَصَرُ خَاسِئًا <mark>وَهُوَ حَسِيرٌ</mark> ﴿٤﴾ وَلَقَدْ زَيَّنَّا السَّمَاءَ الدُّنْيَا بِمَصَابِيحَ وَجَعَلْنَاهَا رُجُومًا لِّلشَّيَاطِينِ ۖ وَأَعْتَدْنَا لَهُمْ عَذَابَ السَّعِيرِ ﴿٥﴾ وَلِلَّذِينَ كَفَرُوا بِرَبِّهِمْ عَذَابُ جَهَنَّمَ ۖ وَبِئْسَ الْمَصِيرُ ﴿٦﴾

CHAPTER 2
Surah Kahf

Ayah 1

Date: _____

Accompanying Video
N/A

Learning Goals
- Apply understanding of grammar to words and fragments
- Memorize vocabulary and translate the ayah

ٱلْحَمْدُ لِلَّهِ ٱلَّذِي أَنزَلَ عَلَىٰ عَبْدِهِ ٱلْكِتَٰبَ وَلَمْ يَجْعَل لَّهُۥ عِوَجَا ۜ ۝١

Four properties: _____

Translation: _____

ٱلْحَمْدُ لِلَّهِ ٱلَّذِي أَنزَلَ عَلَىٰ عَبْدِهِ ٱلْكِتَٰبَ وَلَمْ يَجْعَل لَّهُۥ عِوَجَا ۜ ۝١

Fragment: *Idhaafah*   *Harf Jarr*   *Harf Nasb*   *Mawsoof Sifah*   *Ism Ishara*
(Circle one)

Fragment breakdown: _____   _____

                               (Mudhaaf Ilayh / Victim   (Mudhaaf / Harf Jarr / Harf Nasb
                               Sifah / Mushaar Ilayh)   Mawsoof / Ism Ishara)

Translation: _____

ٱلْحَمْدُ لِلَّهِ ٱلَّذِي أَنزَلَ عَلَىٰ عَبْدِهِ ٱلْكِتَٰبَ وَلَمْ يَجْعَل لَّهُۥ عِوَجَا ۜ ۝١

Four properties: **Jarr,** _____

Translation: _____

Bayyinah Institute • Chapter 2   195

Date: _____

ٱلْحَمْدُ لِلَّهِ ٱلَّذِي أَنزَلَ عَلَىٰ عَبْدِهِ ٱلْكِتَٰبَ وَلَمْ يَجْعَل لَّهُۥ عِوَجَا ۜ ﴿١﴾

Translation: _____

ٱلْحَمْدُ لِلَّهِ ٱلَّذِي أَنزَلَ عَلَىٰ عَبْدِهِ ٱلْكِتَٰبَ وَلَمْ يَجْعَل لَّهُۥ عِوَجَا ۜ ﴿١﴾

First fragment: *Idhaafah*   *Harf Jarr*   *Harf Nasb*   *Mawsoof Sifah*   *Ism Ishara*
(Circle one)

Fragment breakdown: _____ _____
                       (Mudhaaf Ilayh / Victim   (Mudhaaf / Harf Jarr / Harf Nasb
                        Sifah / Mushaar Ilayh)   Mawsoof / Ism Ishara)

Second fragment: *Idhaafah*   *Harf Jarr*   *Harf Nasb*   *Mawsoof Sifah*   *Ism Ishara*
(Circle one)

Fragment breakdown: _____ _____
                       (Mudhaaf Ilayh / Victim   (Mudhaaf / Harf Jarr / Harf Nasb
                        Sifah / Mushaar Ilayh)   Mawsoof / Ism Ishara)

Translation: _____

ٱلْحَمْدُ لِلَّهِ ٱلَّذِي أَنزَلَ عَلَىٰ عَبْدِهِ ٱلْكِتَٰبَ وَلَمْ يَجْعَل لَّهُۥ عِوَجَا ۜ ﴿١﴾

Four properties: _____

Translation: _____

ٱلْحَمْدُ لِلَّهِ ٱلَّذِي أَنزَلَ عَلَىٰ عَبْدِهِ ٱلْكِتَٰبَ وَلَمْ يَجْعَل لَّهُۥ عِوَجَا ۜ ﴿١﴾

Translation: **And** _____

Date: _____

﴿١﴾ ٱلْحَمْدُ لِلَّهِ ٱلَّذِى أَنزَلَ عَلَىٰ عَبْدِهِ ٱلْكِتَٰبَ وَلَمْ يَجْعَل لَّهُۥ عِوَجَا

Translation: _____

﴿١﴾ ٱلْحَمْدُ لِلَّهِ ٱلَّذِى أَنزَلَ عَلَىٰ عَبْدِهِ ٱلْكِتَٰبَ وَلَمْ يَجْعَل لَّهُۥ عِوَجَا

Translation: _____

﴿١﴾ ٱلْحَمْدُ لِلَّهِ ٱلَّذِى أَنزَلَ عَلَىٰ عَبْدِهِ ٱلْكِتَٰبَ وَلَمْ يَجْعَل لَّهُۥ عِوَجَا

Fragment: *Idhaafah*   *Harf Jarr*   *Harf Nasb*   *Mawsoof Sifah*   *Ism Ishara*
(Circle one)

Fragment breakdown: _____   _____
                       (Mudhaaf Ilayh / Victim   (Mudhaaf / Harf Jarr / Harf Nasb
                        Sifah / Mushaar Ilayh)   Mawsoof / Ism Ishara)

Translation: _____

﴿١﴾ ٱلْحَمْدُ لِلَّهِ ٱلَّذِى أَنزَلَ عَلَىٰ عَبْدِهِ ٱلْكِتَٰبَ وَلَمْ يَجْعَل لَّهُۥ عِوَجَا

Four properties: _____

Translation: _____

﴿١﴾ ٱلْحَمْدُ لِلَّهِ ٱلَّذِى أَنزَلَ عَلَىٰ عَبْدِهِ ٱلْكِتَٰبَ وَلَمْ يَجْعَل لَّهُۥ عِوَجَا

Translation: _____

Ayah 2

Learning Goals
- Apply understanding of grammar to words and fragments
- Memorize vocabulary and translate the ayah

Date: _____

Accompanying Video
N/A

قَيِّمًا لِّيُنذِرَ بَأْسًا شَدِيدًا مِّن لَّدُنْهُ

Four properties: _____

Translation: _____

قَيِّمًا لِّيُنذِرَ بَأْسًا شَدِيدًا مِّن لَّدُنْهُ

Translation: _____

قَيِّمًا لِّيُنذِرَ بَأْسًا شَدِيدًا مِّن لَّدُنْهُ

Fragment: Idhaafah   Harf Jarr   Harf Nasb   Mawsoof Sifah   Ism Ishara

Four properties of بَأْسًا: _____

Four properties of شَدِيدًا: _____

Fragment breakdown: _____   _____

Translation: _____

Date: _____

قَيِّمًا لِّيُنذِرَ بَأْسًا شَدِيدًا مِّن لَّدُنْهُ

First fragment: *Idhaafah*   *Harf Jarr*   *Harf Nasb*   *Mawsoof Sifah*   *Ism Ishara*

Fragment breakdown: _____ _____

Second fragment: *Idhaafah*   *Harf Jarr*   *Harf Nasb*   *Mawsoof Sifah*   *Ism Ishara*

Fragment breakdown: _____ _____

Translation: _____

وَيُبَشِّرَ الْمُؤْمِنِينَ الَّذِينَ يَعْمَلُونَ الصَّالِحَاتِ أَنَّ لَهُمْ أَجْرًا حَسَنًا ۝

Translation: And _____

وَيُبَشِّرَ الْمُؤْمِنِينَ الَّذِينَ يَعْمَلُونَ الصَّالِحَاتِ أَنَّ لَهُمْ أَجْرًا حَسَنًا ۝

Translation: _____

وَيُبَشِّرَ الْمُؤْمِنِينَ الَّذِينَ يَعْمَلُونَ الصَّالِحَاتِ أَنَّ لَهُمْ أَجْرًا حَسَنًا ۝

Four properties: _____

Translation: _____

Date: _____

Write the Muslim chart for the word مُؤْمِنٌ:

_____	_____	_____
_____	_____	_____

وَيُبَشِّرَ الْمُؤْمِنِينَ الَّذِينَ يَعْمَلُونَ الصَّالِحَاتِ أَنَّ لَهُمْ أَجْرًا حَسَنًا ۝

Four properties: **Nasb,** _____

Translation: _____

وَيُبَشِّرَ الْمُؤْمِنِينَ الَّذِينَ يَعْمَلُونَ الصَّالِحَاتِ أَنَّ لَهُمْ أَجْرًا حَسَنًا ۝

Translation: _____

وَيُبَشِّرَ الْمُؤْمِنِينَ الَّذِينَ يَعْمَلُونَ الصَّالِحَاتِ أَنَّ لَهُمْ أَجْرًا حَسَنًا ۝

Four properties: _____

Translation: _____

Date: _____

Write the Muslim chart for the word صَالِحٌ:

_____   _____   _____

_____   _____   _____

_____   _____

وَيُبَشِّرَ الْمُؤْمِنِينَ الَّذِينَ يَعْمَلُونَ الصَّالِحَاتِ أَنَّ لَهُمْ أَجْرًا حَسَنًا ۝

Fragment: *Idhaafah*   *Harf Jarr*   *Harf Nasb*   *Mawsoof Sifah*   *Ism Ishara*

Fragment breakdown: _____   _____

Translation: _____

وَيُبَشِّرَ الْمُؤْمِنِينَ الَّذِينَ يَعْمَلُونَ الصَّالِحَاتِ أَنَّ لَهُمْ أَجْرًا حَسَنًا ۝

Fragment: *Idhaafah*   *Harf Jarr*   *Harf Nasb*   *Mawsoof Sifah*   *Ism Ishara*

Four properties of أَجْرًا: _____

Four properties of حَسَنًا: _____

Fragment breakdown: _____   _____

Translation: _____

Date: _____

$$\text{وَيُبَشِّرَ الْمُؤْمِنِينَ الَّذِينَ يَعْمَلُونَ الصَّالِحَاتِ أَنَّ لَهُمْ أَجْرًا حَسَنًا ۝}$$

First fragment: Idhaafah   Harf Jarr   Harf Nasb   Mawsoof Sifah   Ism Ishara

Fragment breakdown: _____

Second fragment: Idhaafah   Harf Jarr   Harf Nasb   Mawsoof Sifah   Ism Ishara

Fragment breakdown: _____

Translation: _____

قَيِّمًا لِّيُنذِرَ بَأْسًا شَدِيدًا مِّن لَّدُنْهُ وَيُبَشِّرَ الْمُؤْمِنِينَ الَّذِينَ يَعْمَلُونَ الصَّالِحَاتِ أَنَّ لَهُمْ أَجْرًا حَسَنًا ۝

Translation: _____

202   Chapter 2 • Bayyinah Institute

Ayah 3-4

Date: _____

Accompanying Video
N/A

Learning Goals
- Apply understanding of grammar to words and fragments
- Memorize vocabulary and translate the ayah

مَّاكِثِينَ فِيهِ أَبَدًا ۝ وَيُنذِرَ الَّذِينَ قَالُوا اتَّخَذَ اللَّهُ وَلَدًا ۝

Four properties: _____

Translation: _____

مَّاكِثِينَ فِيهِ أَبَدًا ۝ وَيُنذِرَ الَّذِينَ قَالُوا اتَّخَذَ اللَّهُ وَلَدًا ۝

Fragment: *Idhaafah*   *Harf Jarr*   *Harf Nasb*   *Mawsoof Sifah*   *Ism Ishara*

Fragment breakdown: _____   _____

Translation: _____

مَّاكِثِينَ فِيهِ أَبَدًا ۝ وَيُنذِرَ الَّذِينَ قَالُوا اتَّخَذَ اللَّهُ وَلَدًا ۝

Four properties: _____

Translation: _____

Bayyinah Institute • Chapter 2

Date: _____

مَّاكِثِينَ فِيهِ أَبَدًا ﴿٣﴾ وَيُنذِرَ الَّذِينَ قَالُوا اتَّخَذَ اللَّهُ وَلَدًا ﴿٤﴾

Translation: _____

مَّاكِثِينَ فِيهِ أَبَدًا ﴿٣﴾ وَيُنذِرَ الَّذِينَ قَالُوا اتَّخَذَ اللَّهُ وَلَدًا ﴿٤﴾

Translation: _____

مَّاكِثِينَ فِيهِ أَبَدًا ﴿٣﴾ وَيُنذِرَ الَّذِينَ قَالُوا اتَّخَذَ اللَّهُ وَلَدًا ﴿٤﴾

Four properties: Nasb, _____

Translation: _____

Write the Ism Mawsool chart:

_____   _____   _____

_____   _____   _____

مَّاكِثِينَ فِيهِ أَبَدًا ﴿٣﴾ وَيُنذِرَ الَّذِينَ قَالُوا اتَّخَذَ اللَّهُ وَلَدًا ﴿٤﴾

Translation: _____

مَّاكِثِينَ فِيهِ أَبَدًا ﴿٣﴾ وَيُنذِرَ الَّذِينَ قَالُوا اتَّخَذَ اللَّهُ وَلَدًا ﴿٤﴾

Translation: _____

Date: _____

مَّاكِثِينَ فِيهِ أَبَدًا ﴿٣﴾ وَيُنذِرَ الَّذِينَ قَالُوا اتَّخَذَ ‎**اللَّهُ**‎ وَلَدًا ﴿٤﴾

Four properties: _____

Translation: _____

مَّاكِثِينَ فِيهِ أَبَدًا ﴿٣﴾ وَيُنذِرَ الَّذِينَ قَالُوا اتَّخَذَ اللَّهُ ‎**وَلَدًا**‎ ﴿٤﴾

Four properties: _____

Translation: _____

مَّاكِثِينَ فِيهِ أَبَدًا ﴿٣﴾ وَيُنذِرَ الَّذِينَ قَالُوا اتَّخَذَ اللَّهُ وَلَدًا ﴿٤﴾

Translation: _____

Bayyinah Institute • Chapter 2 • 205

Ayah 5

Learning Goals
- Apply understanding of grammar to words and fragments
- Memorize vocabulary and translate the ayah

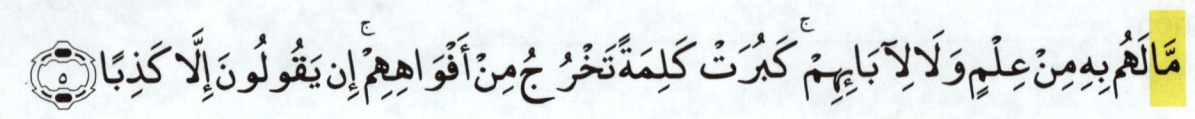

Date: _____

Accompanying Video
N/A

مَّا لَهُم بِهِۦ مِنْ عِلْمٍ وَلَا لِآبَآئِهِمْ ۚ كَبُرَتْ كَلِمَةً تَخْرُجُ مِنْ أَفْوَاهِهِمْ ۚ إِن يَقُولُونَ إِلَّا كَذِبًا ۝

Translation: **Not** _____

مَّا لَهُم بِهِۦ مِنْ عِلْمٍ وَلَا لِآبَآئِهِمْ ۚ كَبُرَتْ كَلِمَةً تَخْرُجُ مِنْ أَفْوَاهِهِمْ ۚ إِن يَقُولُونَ إِلَّا كَذِبًا ۝

Fragment: *Idhaafah*   *Harf Jarr*   *Harf Nasb*   *Mawsoof Sifah*   *Ism Ishara*

Fragment breakdown: _____ _____

Translation: _____

مَّا لَهُم بِهِۦ مِنْ عِلْمٍ وَلَا لِآبَآئِهِمْ ۚ كَبُرَتْ كَلِمَةً تَخْرُجُ مِنْ أَفْوَاهِهِمْ ۚ إِن يَقُولُونَ إِلَّا كَذِبًا ۝

Fragment: *Idhaafah*   *Harf Jarr*   *Harf Nasb*   *Mawsoof Sifah*   *Ism Ishara*

Fragment breakdown: _____ _____

Translation: _____

Date: _____

مَّا لَهُم بِهِۦ مِنْ عِلْمٍ وَلَا لِآبَآئِهِمْ ۚ كَبُرَتْ كَلِمَةً تَخْرُجُ مِنْ أَفْوَاهِهِمْ ۚ إِن يَقُولُونَ إِلَّا كَذِبًا ۝

Fragment: *Idhaafah*   *Harf Jarr*   *Harf Nasb*   *Mawsoof Sifah*   *Ism Ishara*

Fragment breakdown: _____   _____

Translation: _____

مَّا لَهُم بِهِۦ مِنْ عِلْمٍ وَلَا لِآبَآئِهِمْ ۚ كَبُرَتْ كَلِمَةً تَخْرُجُ مِنْ أَفْوَاهِهِمْ ۚ إِن يَقُولُونَ إِلَّا كَذِبًا ۝

Translation: _____

مَّا لَهُم بِهِۦ مِنْ عِلْمٍ وَلَا لِآبَآئِهِمْ ۚ كَبُرَتْ كَلِمَةً تَخْرُجُ مِنْ أَفْوَاهِهِمْ ۚ إِن يَقُولُونَ إِلَّا كَذِبًا ۝

Translation: _____

مَّا لَهُم بِهِۦ مِنْ عِلْمٍ وَلَا لِآبَآئِهِمْ ۚ كَبُرَتْ كَلِمَةً تَخْرُجُ مِنْ أَفْوَاهِهِمْ ۚ إِن يَقُولُونَ إِلَّا كَذِبًا ۝

First fragment: *Idhaafah*   *Harf Jarr*   *Harf Nasb*   *Mawsoof Sifah*   *Ism Ishara*

Fragment breakdown: _____   _____

Second fragment: *Idhaafah*   *Harf Jarr*   *Harf Nasb*   *Mawsoof Sifah*   *Ism Ishara*

Fragment breakdown: _____

Translation: _____

Date: _____

مَّا لَهُم بِهِۦ مِنْ عِلْمٍ وَلَا لِآبَآئِهِمْ ۚ **كَبُرَتْ** كَلِمَةً تَخْرُجُ مِنْ أَفْوَٰهِهِمْ ۚ إِن يَقُولُونَ إِلَّا كَذِبًا ۝

Translation: _____

مَّا لَهُم بِهِۦ مِنْ عِلْمٍ وَلَا لِآبَآئِهِمْ ۚ كَبُرَتْ **كَلِمَةً** تَخْرُجُ مِنْ أَفْوَٰهِهِمْ ۚ إِن يَقُولُونَ إِلَّا كَذِبًا ۝

Four properties: _____

Translation: _____

مَّا لَهُم بِهِۦ مِنْ عِلْمٍ وَلَا لِآبَآئِهِمْ ۚ كَبُرَتْ كَلِمَةً **تَخْرُجُ** مِنْ أَفْوَٰهِهِمْ ۚ إِن يَقُولُونَ إِلَّا كَذِبًا ۝

Translation: _____

مَّا لَهُم بِهِۦ مِنْ عِلْمٍ وَلَا لِآبَآئِهِمْ ۚ كَبُرَتْ كَلِمَةً تَخْرُجُ **مِنْ أَفْوَٰهِهِمْ** ۚ إِن يَقُولُونَ إِلَّا كَذِبًا ۝

First fragment: *Idhaafah*   *Harf Jarr*   *Harf Nasb*   *Mawsoof Sifah*   *Ism Ishara*

Fragment breakdown: _____   _____

Second fragment: *Idhaafah*   *Harf Jarr*   *Harf Nasb*   *Mawsoof Sifah*   *Ism Ishara*

Fragment breakdown: _____   _____

Translation: _____

208   Chapter 2 • Bayyinah Institute

Date: _____

مَّا لَهُم بِهِۦ مِنْ عِلْمٍ وَلَا لِءَابَآئِهِمْ ۚ كَبُرَتْ كَلِمَةً تَخْرُجُ مِنْ أَفْوَٰهِهِمْ ۚ إِن يَقُولُونَ إِلَّا كَذِبًا ۝

Translation: Not _____

مَّا لَهُم بِهِۦ مِنْ عِلْمٍ وَلَا لِءَابَآئِهِمْ ۚ كَبُرَتْ كَلِمَةً تَخْرُجُ مِنْ أَفْوَٰهِهِمْ ۚ إِن يَقُولُونَ إِلَّا كَذِبًا ۝

Translation: _____

مَّا لَهُم بِهِۦ مِنْ عِلْمٍ وَلَا لِءَابَآئِهِمْ ۚ كَبُرَتْ كَلِمَةً تَخْرُجُ مِنْ أَفْوَٰهِهِمْ ۚ إِن يَقُولُونَ إِلَّا كَذِبًا ۝

Translation: Except _____

مَّا لَهُم بِهِۦ مِنْ عِلْمٍ وَلَا لِءَابَآئِهِمْ ۚ كَبُرَتْ كَلِمَةً تَخْرُجُ مِنْ أَفْوَٰهِهِمْ ۚ إِن يَقُولُونَ إِلَّا كَذِبًا ۝

Four properties: _____

Translation: _____

مَّا لَهُم بِهِۦ مِنْ عِلْمٍ وَلَا لِءَابَآئِهِمْ ۚ كَبُرَتْ كَلِمَةً تَخْرُجُ مِنْ أَفْوَٰهِهِمْ ۚ إِن يَقُولُونَ إِلَّا كَذِبًا ۝

Translation: _____

Ayah 6

Date: _____

Accompanying Video
N/A

Learning Goals
- Apply understanding of grammar to words and fragments
- Memorize vocabulary and translate the ayah

فَلَعَلَّكَ بَاخِعٌ نَفْسَكَ عَلَىٰ آثَارِهِمْ إِن لَّمْ يُؤْمِنُوا بِهَٰذَا الْحَدِيثِ أَسَفًا ﴿٦﴾

Translation: So _____

فَلَعَلَّكَ بَاخِعٌ نَفْسَكَ عَلَىٰ آثَارِهِمْ إِن لَّمْ يُؤْمِنُوا بِهَٰذَا الْحَدِيثِ أَسَفًا ﴿٦﴾

Fragment: *Idhaafah*   *Harf Jarr*   *Harf Nasb*   *Mawsoof Sifah*   *Ism Ishara*

Fragment breakdown: _____   _____

Translation: _____

فَلَعَلَّكَ بَاخِعٌ نَفْسَكَ عَلَىٰ آثَارِهِمْ إِن لَّمْ يُؤْمِنُوا بِهَٰذَا الْحَدِيثِ أَسَفًا ﴿٦﴾

Four properties: _____

Translation: _____

210 Chapter 2 • Bayyinah Institute

Date: _____

فَلَعَلَّكَ بَاخِعٌ <mark>نَّفْسَكَ</mark> عَلَىٰ آثَارِهِمْ إِن لَّمْ يُؤْمِنُوا بِهَـٰذَا الْحَدِيثِ أَسَفًا ﴿٦﴾

Fragment: *Idhaafah*   *Harf Jarr*   *Harf Nasb*   *Mawsoof Sifah*   *Ism Ishara*

Fragment breakdown: _____   _____

Translation: _____

فَلَعَلَّكَ بَاخِعٌ نَّفْسَكَ <mark>عَلَىٰ آثَارِهِمْ</mark> إِن لَّمْ يُؤْمِنُوا بِهَـٰذَا الْحَدِيثِ أَسَفًا ﴿٦﴾

First fragment: *Idhaafah*   *Harf Jarr*   *Harf Nasb*   *Mawsoof Sifah*   *Ism Ishara*

Fragment breakdown: _____   _____

Second fragment: *Idhaafah*   *Harf Jarr*   *Harf Nasb*   *Mawsoof Sifah*   *Ism Ishara*

Fragment breakdown: _____   _____

Translation: _____

فَلَعَلَّكَ بَاخِعٌ نَّفْسَكَ عَلَىٰ آثَارِهِمْ <mark>إِن لَّمْ</mark> يُؤْمِنُوا بِهَـٰذَا الْحَدِيثِ أَسَفًا ﴿٦﴾

Translation: _____

فَلَعَلَّكَ بَاخِعٌ نَّفْسَكَ عَلَىٰ آثَارِهِمْ إِن <mark>لَّمْ</mark> يُؤْمِنُوا بِهَـٰذَا الْحَدِيثِ أَسَفًا ﴿٦﴾

Translation: _____

Bayyinah Institute • Chapter 2

Date: _____

فَلَعَلَّكَ بَاخِعٌ نَفْسَكَ عَلَىٰ آثَارِهِمْ إِن لَّمْ يُؤْمِنُوا بِهَٰذَا الْحَدِيثِ أَسَفًا ﴿٦﴾

Translation: _____

فَلَعَلَّكَ بَاخِعٌ نَفْسَكَ عَلَىٰ آثَارِهِمْ إِن لَّمْ يُؤْمِنُوا بِهَٰذَا الْحَدِيثِ أَسَفًا ﴿٦﴾

First fragment: Idhaafah   Harf Jarr   Harf Nasb   Mawsoof Sifah   Ism Ishara

Fragment breakdown: _____   _____

Second fragment: Idhaafah   Harf Jarr   Harf Nasb   Mawsoof Sifah   Ism Ishara

Fragment breakdown: _____   _____

Translation: _____

فَلَعَلَّكَ بَاخِعٌ نَفْسَكَ عَلَىٰ آثَارِهِمْ إِن لَّمْ يُؤْمِنُوا بِهَٰذَا الْحَدِيثِ أَسَفًا ﴿٦﴾

Four properties: _____

Translation: _____

فَلَعَلَّكَ بَاخِعٌ نَفْسَكَ عَلَىٰ آثَارِهِمْ إِن لَّمْ يُؤْمِنُوا بِهَٰذَا الْحَدِيثِ أَسَفًا ﴿٦﴾

Translation:

Ayah 7

Date: _____

Accompanying Video
N/A

Learning Goals
- Apply understanding of grammar to words and fragments
- Memorize vocabulary and translate the ayah

إِنَّا جَعَلْنَا مَا عَلَى الْأَرْضِ زِينَةً لَّهَا لِنَبْلُوَهُمْ أَيُّهُمْ أَحْسَنُ عَمَلًا ﴿٧﴾

Fragment: Idhaafah   Harf Jarr   Harf Nasb   Mawsoof Sifah   Ism Ishara

Fragment breakdown: _____   _____

Translation: _____

إِنَّا جَعَلْنَا مَا عَلَى الْأَرْضِ زِينَةً لَّهَا لِنَبْلُوَهُمْ أَيُّهُمْ أَحْسَنُ عَمَلًا ﴿٧﴾

Translation: _____

إِنَّا جَعَلْنَا مَا عَلَى الْأَرْضِ زِينَةً لَّهَا لِنَبْلُوَهُمْ أَيُّهُمْ أَحْسَنُ عَمَلًا ﴿٧﴾

Translation: What

إِنَّا جَعَلْنَا مَا عَلَى الْأَرْضِ زِينَةً لَّهَا لِنَبْلُوَهُمْ أَيُّهُمْ أَحْسَنُ عَمَلًا ﴿٧﴾

Fragment: Idhaafah   Harf Jarr   Harf Nasb   Mawsoof Sifah   Ism Ishara

Fragment breakdown: _____   _____

Translation: _____

Bayyinah Institute • Chapter 2

Date: _____

$$\text{إِنَّا جَعَلْنَا عَلَى الْأَرْضِ زِينَةً لَّهَا لِنَبْلُوَهُمْ أَيُّهُمْ أَحْسَنُ عَمَلًا ﴿٧﴾}$$

Four properties: _____

Translation: _____

$$\text{إِنَّا جَعَلْنَا عَلَى الْأَرْضِ زِينَةً لَّهَا لِنَبْلُوَهُمْ أَيُّهُمْ أَحْسَنُ عَمَلًا ﴿٧﴾}$$

Fragment: Idhaafah   Harf Jarr   Harf Nasb   Mawsoof Sifah   Ism Ishara

Fragment breakdown: _____   _____

Translation: _____

$$\text{إِنَّا جَعَلْنَا عَلَى الْأَرْضِ زِينَةً لَّهَا لِنَبْلُوَهُمْ أَيُّهُمْ أَحْسَنُ عَمَلًا ﴿٧﴾}$$

Translation: _____

$$\text{إِنَّا جَعَلْنَا عَلَى الْأَرْضِ زِينَةً لَّهَا لِنَبْلُوَهُمْ أَيُّهُمْ أَحْسَنُ عَمَلًا ﴿٧﴾}$$

Fragment: Idhaafah   Harf Jarr   Harf Nasb   Mawsoof Sifah   Ism Ishara

Fragment breakdown: _____   _____

Translation: _____

Date: _____

إِنَّا جَعَلْنَا مَا عَلَى الْأَرْضِ زِينَةً لَّهَا لِنَبْلُوَهُمْ أَيُّهُمْ أَحْسَنُ عَمَلًا ۝

Four properties: _____

Translation: _____

إِنَّا جَعَلْنَا مَا عَلَى الْأَرْضِ زِينَةً لَّهَا لِنَبْلُوَهُمْ أَيُّهُمْ أَحْسَنُ عَمَلًا ۝

Four properties: _____

Translation: _____

إِنَّا جَعَلْنَا مَا عَلَى الْأَرْضِ زِينَةً لَّهَا لِنَبْلُوَهُمْ أَيُّهُمْ أَحْسَنُ عَمَلًا ۝

Translation: _____

Ayah 8

Date: _____

Accompanying Video
N/A

Learning Goals
- Apply understanding of grammar to words and fragments
- Memorize vocabulary and translate the ayah

وَإِنَّا لَجَاعِلُونَ مَا عَلَيْهَا صَعِيدًا جُرُزًا ۝

Translation: _____

وَإِنَّا لَجَاعِلُونَ مَا عَلَيْهَا صَعِيدًا جُرُزًا ۝

Fragment: Idhaafah   Harf Jarr   Harf Nasb   Mawsoof Sifah   Ism Ishara

Fragment breakdown: _____ _____

Translation: _____

وَإِنَّا لَجَاعِلُونَ مَا عَلَيْهَا صَعِيدًا جُرُزًا ۝

Translation: **No doubt** _____

وَإِنَّا لَجَاعِلُونَ مَا عَلَيْهَا صَعِيدًا جُرُزًا ۝

Four properties: _____

Translation: _____

216   Chapter 2 • Bayyinah Institute

Write the Muslim chart for the word جَاعِلٌ:

_____   _____   _____

_____   _____   _____

_____   _____   _____

وَإِنَّا لَجَاعِلُونَ مَا عَلَيْهَا صَعِيدًا جُرُزًا ﴿٨﴾

Translation: **What** _____

وَإِنَّا لَجَاعِلُونَ مَا عَلَيْهَا صَعِيدًا جُرُزًا ﴿٨﴾

Fragment: *Idhaafah   Harf Jarr   Harf Nasb   Mawsoof Sifah   Ism Ishara*

Fragment breakdown: _____   _____

Translation: _____

Bayyinah Institute • Chapter 2

وَإِنَّا لَجَاعِلُونَ مَا عَلَيْهَا صَعِيدًا جُرُزًا ﴿٨﴾

Fragment: Idhaafah   Harf Jarr   Harf Nasb   Mawsoof Sifah   Ism Ishara

Four properties of صَعِيدًا: _____

Four properties of جُرُزًا: _____

Fragment breakdown: _____   _____

Translation: _____

وَإِنَّا لَجَاعِلُونَ مَا عَلَيْهَا صَعِيدًا جُرُزًا ﴿٨﴾

Translation: _____

Ayah 9

Learning Goals
- Apply understanding of grammar to words and fragments
- Memorize vocabulary and translate the ayah

Accompanying Video
N/A

أَمْ حَسِبْتَ أَنَّ أَصْحَابَ الْكَهْفِ وَالرَّقِيمِ كَانُوا مِنْ آيَاتِنَا عَجَبًا ۝

Translation: Or _____

أَمْ حَسِبْتَ أَنَّ أَصْحَابَ الْكَهْفِ وَالرَّقِيمِ كَانُوا مِنْ آيَاتِنَا عَجَبًا ۝

Translation: _____

أَمْ حَسِبْتَ أَنَّ أَصْحَابَ الْكَهْفِ وَالرَّقِيمِ كَانُوا مِنْ آيَاتِنَا عَجَبًا ۝

Fragment: Idhaafah   Harf Jarr   Harf Nasb   Mawsoof Sifah   Ism Ishara

Fragment breakdown: _____ _____

Translation: _____

Date: _____

﴿أَمْ حَسِبْتَ أَنَّ أَصْحَابَ الْكَهْفِ وَالرَّقِيمِ كَانُوا مِنْ آيَاتِنَا عَجَبًا ۝﴾

Fragment: *Idhaafah*   *Harf Jarr*   *Harf Nasb*   *Mawsoof Sifah*   *Ism Ishara*

Fragment breakdown: _____   _____

Translation: _____

﴿أَمْ حَسِبْتَ أَنَّ أَصْحَابَ الْكَهْفِ وَالرَّقِيمِ كَانُوا مِنْ آيَاتِنَا عَجَبًا ۝﴾

First fragment: *Idhaafah*   *Harf Jarr*   *Harf Nasb*   *Mawsoof Sifah*   *Ism Ishara*

Four properties of أَصْحَابَ: _____

Fragment breakdown: _____   _____

Second fragment: *Idhaafah*   *Harf Jarr*   *Harf Nasb*   *Mawsoof Sifah*   *Ism Ishara*

Four properties of الْكَهْفِ: _____

Four properties of الرَّقِيم: _____

Fragment breakdown: _____   _____

Translation: _____

Date: _____

أَمْ حَسِبْتَ أَنَّ أَصْحَابَ الْكَهْفِ وَالرَّقِيمِ **كَانُوا** مِنْ آيَاتِنَا عَجَبًا ﴿٩﴾

Translation: _____

أَمْ حَسِبْتَ أَنَّ أَصْحَابَ الْكَهْفِ وَالرَّقِيمِ كَانُوا **مِنْ آيَاتِنَا** عَجَبًا ﴿٩﴾

First fragment: Idhaafah   Harf Jarr   Harf Nasb   Mawsoof Sifah   Ism Ishara

Fragment breakdown: _____   _____

Second fragment: Idhaafah   Harf Jarr   Harf Nasb   Mawsoof Sifah   Ism Ishara

Fragment breakdown: _____   _____

Translation: _____

أَمْ حَسِبْتَ أَنَّ أَصْحَابَ الْكَهْفِ وَالرَّقِيمِ كَانُوا مِنْ آيَاتِنَا **عَجَبًا** ﴿٩﴾

Four properties: _____

Translation: _____

أَمْ حَسِبْتَ أَنَّ أَصْحَابَ الْكَهْفِ وَالرَّقِيمِ كَانُوا مِنْ آيَاتِنَا عَجَبًا ﴿٩﴾

Translation: _____

Ayah 10

Learning Goals
- Apply understanding of grammar to words and fragments
- Memorize vocabulary and translate the ayah

Accompanying Video
N/A

Date: _____

﴿١٠﴾ إِذْ أَوَى الْفِتْيَةُ إِلَى الْكَهْفِ فَقَالُوا رَبَّنَا آتِنَا مِن لَّدُنكَ رَحْمَةً وَهَيِّئْ لَنَا مِنْ أَمْرِنَا رَشَدًا

Translation: _____

﴿١٠﴾ إِذْ أَوَى الْفِتْيَةُ إِلَى الْكَهْفِ فَقَالُوا رَبَّنَا آتِنَا مِن لَّدُنكَ رَحْمَةً وَهَيِّئْ لَنَا مِنْ أَمْرِنَا رَشَدًا

Translation: _____

﴿١٠﴾ إِذْ أَوَى الْفِتْيَةُ إِلَى الْكَهْفِ فَقَالُوا رَبَّنَا آتِنَا مِن لَّدُنكَ رَحْمَةً وَهَيِّئْ لَنَا مِنْ أَمْرِنَا رَشَدًا

Four properties: _____

Translation: _____

﴿١٠﴾ إِذْ أَوَى الْفِتْيَةُ إِلَى الْكَهْفِ فَقَالُوا رَبَّنَا آتِنَا مِن لَّدُنكَ رَحْمَةً وَهَيِّئْ لَنَا مِنْ أَمْرِنَا رَشَدًا

Fragment: Idhaafah   Harf Jarr   Harf Nasb   Mawsoof Sifah   Ism Ishara

Fragment breakdown: _____   _____

Translation: _____

Date: _____

إِذْ أَوَى الْفِتْيَةُ إِلَى الْكَهْفِ **فَ**قَالُوا رَبَّنَا آتِنَا مِن لَّدُنكَ رَحْمَةً وَهَيِّئْ لَنَا مِنْ أَمْرِنَا رَشَدًا ﴿١٠﴾

Translation: So _____

إِذْ أَوَى الْفِتْيَةُ إِلَى الْكَهْفِ فَ**قَالُوا** رَبَّنَا آتِنَا مِن لَّدُنكَ رَحْمَةً وَهَيِّئْ لَنَا مِنْ أَمْرِنَا رَشَدًا ﴿١٠﴾

Translation: _____

إِذْ أَوَى الْفِتْيَةُ إِلَى الْكَهْفِ فَقَالُوا **رَبَّنَا** آتِنَا مِن لَّدُنكَ رَحْمَةً وَهَيِّئْ لَنَا مِنْ أَمْرِنَا رَشَدًا ﴿١٠﴾

Fragment: *Idhaafah*   *Harf Jarr*   *Harf Nasb*   *Mawsoof Sifah*   *Ism Ishara*

Fragment breakdown: _____

Translation: _____

إِذْ أَوَى الْفِتْيَةُ إِلَى الْكَهْفِ فَقَالُوا رَبَّنَا **آتِنَا** مِن لَّدُنكَ رَحْمَةً وَهَيِّئْ لَنَا مِنْ أَمْرِنَا رَشَدًا ﴿١٠﴾

Translation: _____

Bayyinah Institute • Chapter 2

Date: _____

إِذْ أَوَى الْفِتْيَةُ إِلَى الْكَهْفِ فَقَالُوا رَبَّنَا آتِنَا مِن لَّدُنكَ رَحْمَةً وَهَيِّئْ لَنَا مِنْ أَمْرِنَا رَشَدًا ﴿١٠﴾

First fragment: Idhaafah   Harf Jarr   Harf Nasb   Mawsoof Sifah   Ism Ishara

Fragment breakdown: _____   _____

Second fragment: Idhaafah   Harf Jarr   Harf Nasb   Mawsoof Sifah   Ism Ishara

Fragment breakdown: _____

Translation: _____

إِذْ أَوَى الْفِتْيَةُ إِلَى الْكَهْفِ فَقَالُوا رَبَّنَا آتِنَا مِن لَّدُنكَ رَحْمَةً وَهَيِّئْ لَنَا مِنْ أَمْرِنَا رَشَدًا ﴿١٠﴾

Four properties: _____

Translation: _____

إِذْ أَوَى الْفِتْيَةُ إِلَى الْكَهْفِ فَقَالُوا رَبَّنَا آتِنَا مِن لَّدُنكَ رَحْمَةً وَهَيِّئْ لَنَا مِنْ أَمْرِنَا رَشَدًا ﴿١٠﴾

Translation: _____

إِذْ أَوَى الْفِتْيَةُ إِلَى الْكَهْفِ فَقَالُوا رَبَّنَا آتِنَا مِن لَّدُنكَ رَحْمَةً وَهَيِّئْ لَنَا مِنْ أَمْرِنَا رَشَدًا ﴿١٠﴾

Translation: _____

Date: _____

إِذْ أَوَى الْفِتْيَةُ إِلَى الْكَهْفِ فَقَالُوا رَبَّنَا آتِنَا مِن لَّدُنكَ رَحْمَةً وَهَيِّئْ **لَنَا** مِنْ أَمْرِنَا رَشَدًا ﴿١٠﴾

Fragment: *Idhaafah*   *Harf Jarr*   *Harf Nasb*   *Mawsoof Sifah*   *Ism Ishara*

Fragment breakdown: _____   _____

Translation: _____

إِذْ أَوَى الْفِتْيَةُ إِلَى الْكَهْفِ فَقَالُوا رَبَّنَا آتِنَا مِن لَّدُنكَ رَحْمَةً وَهَيِّئْ لَنَا **مِنْ أَمْرِ** نَا رَشَدًا ﴿١٠﴾

First fragment: *Idhaafah*   *Harf Jarr*   *Harf Nasb*   *Mawsoof Sifah*   *Ism Ishara*

Fragment breakdown: _____   _____

Second fragment: *Idhaafah*   *Harf Jarr*   *Harf Nasb*   *Mawsoof Sifah*   *Ism Ishara*

Fragment breakdown: _____   _____

Translation: _____

إِذْ أَوَى الْفِتْيَةُ إِلَى الْكَهْفِ فَقَالُوا رَبَّنَا آتِنَا مِن لَّدُنكَ رَحْمَةً وَهَيِّئْ لَنَا مِنْ أَمْرِنَا **رَشَدًا** ﴿١٠﴾

Four properties: _____

Translation: _____

Bayyinah Institute • Chapter 2   225

Date: _____

إِذْ أَوَى الْفِتْيَةُ إِلَى الْكَهْفِ فَقَالُوا رَبَّنَا آتِنَا مِن لَّدُنكَ رَحْمَةً وَهَيِّئْ لَنَا مِنْ أَمْرِنَا رَشَدًا ﴿١٠﴾

Translation: _____
_____